DRAMA CLASS

CW00421377

The Drama Classics ser
plays in affordable pape
and theatregoers. The h
introductions, uncluttered texts and an overall theatrical
perspective.

Given that readers may be encountering a particular play for
the first time, the introduction seeks to fill in the theatrical/
historical background and to outline the chief themes rather
than concentrate on interpretational and textual analysis.
Similarly the play-texts themselves are free of footnotes and
other interpolations: instead there is an end-glossary of
'difficult' words and phrases.

The texts of the English-language plays in the series
have been prepared taking full account of all existing
scholarship. The foreign-language plays have been newly
translated into a modern English that is both actable and
accurate: many of the translators regularly have their work
staged professionally.

Edited until his early death by Kenneth McLeish, the Drama
Classics series continues with his aim of providing a first-class
library of dramatic literature representing the best of world
theatre.

Associate editors:
Professor Trevor R. Griffiths
Dr. Colin Counsell
School of Arts and Humanities
University of North London

DRAMA CLASSICS *the first hundred*

The Alchemist
All for Love
Andromache
Antigone
Arden of Faversham
Bacchae
Bartholomew Fair
The Beaux Stratagem
The Beggar's Opera
Birds
Celestina
The Changeling
A Chaste Maid in Cheapside
The Cherry Orchard
Children of the Sun
El Cid
The Country Wife
The Dance of Death
The Devil is an Ass
Doctor Faustus
A Doll's House
Don Juan
The Duchess of Malfi
Edward II
Electra (Euripides)
Electra (Sophocles)
An Enemy of the People
Every Man in his Humour
Everyman
Faust
A Flea in her Ear
Frogs
Fuenteovejuna
The Game of Love and Chance
Ghosts
The Government Inspector

Hecuba
Hedda Gabler
The Hypochondriac
The Importance of Being Earnest
An Ideal Husband
An Italian Straw Hat
The Jew of Malta
The Knight of the Burning Pestle
The Lady from the Sea
The Learned Ladies
Lady Windermere's Fan
Life is a Dream
The Lower Depths
The Lucky Chance
Lulu
Lysistrata
The Magistrate
The Malcontent
The Man of Mode
The Marriage of Figaro
Mary Stuart
The Master Builder
Medea
The Misanthrope
The Miser
Miss Julie
A Month in the Country
A New Way to Pay Old Debts
Oedipus
The Oresteia
Peer Gynt
Phedra
The Playboy of the Western World
The Recruiting Officer

The Revenger's Tragedy
The Rivals
The Roaring Girl
La Ronde
Rosmersholm
The Rover
Scapino
The School for Scandal
The Seagull
The Servant of Two Masters
She Stoops to Conquer
The Shoemakers' Holiday
Six Characters in Search of an Author
The Spanish Tragedy
Spring's Awakening
Summerfolk
Tartuffe
Three Sisters
'Tis Pity She's a Whore
Too Clever by Half
Ubu
Uncle Vanya
Volpone
The Way of the World
The White Devil
The Wild Duck
A Woman of No Importance
Women Beware Women
Women of Troy
Woyzeck

The publishers welcome suggestions for further titles

DRAMA CLASSICS

AN ITALIAN STRAW HAT

by

Eugène Labiche and Marc-Michel

translated and introduced by
Kenneth McLeish

NICK HERN BOOKS

London

www.nickhernbooks.co.uk

A Drama Classic

An Italian Straw Hat first published in Great Britain in this translation as a paperback original in 1996 by Nick Hern Books Limited, 14 Larden Road, London W3 7ST

Reprinted 2006

Typeset by Country Setting, Kingsdown, Kent CT14 8ES
Printed and bound in Great Britain by Biddles, King's Lynn

A CIP catalogue record for this book is available from
the British Library

ISBN-13   978 1 85459 300 9
ISBN-10   1 85459 300 5

Introduction

Eugène-Marin Labiche (1815-88)

Labiche's father manufactured glucose syrup, which was widely used both for cooking and as a drink (diluted with fruit-juice or water: the 'sugar-water' which people in *An Italian Straw Hat* drink so enthusiastically). The family was well-to-do without being rich and belonged precisely to the comfortable middle-class Labiche was later to satirise so uproariously. The boy was conventionally educated – his only intellectual gift, he later claimed, was a photographic memory which allowed him to pass exams by quoting textbooks verbatim – and he followed his parents' wishes so far as to enrol for a law degree. But from the age of 18 he had begun to write, and after a few false starts (travel journalism, a novel, theatre criticism), he delivered his first play in 1837, and his career was set.

In the next 38 years Labiche wrote so many plays, scenes and sketches that he himself found it hard to remember them all. The 'Complete Works: Series One' he published in ten volumes in 1878-9 (as part of a campaign to be the first farce-writer given France's highest literary honour, election to the Académie française) contains 57 plays, and scholars have tracked down another 107 (usually of less worth) to which his name can be definitely assigned. Following the custom of the time, he generally worked with at least one collaborator, and rewrote and revised during rehearsals and even – when plays were successful – during the runs themselves.

Like many theatre writers before and since, Labiche professed to hate the stage and everything to do with it. He used his royalties to buy a 500-hectare estate at Souvigny, some 120km South of Paris, and lived the life of a country farmer, spending half of each year there and travelling to Paris only for rehearsals. (He was a devotee of that recent development, the railway, and train-travel was one of his passions.) He spent time in local politics, and counted his election as Mayor of Souvigny in 1868 as one of the greatest moments of his life, equal to his election to the Académie française (1880) or the day when he saw his beloved son André graduate as Bachelor of Law.

A lover of good living – he once wrote that his cook and wine-cellar in Souvigny brought him far more pleasure than any of his plays – Labiche began to suffer serious health-problems in his mid-sixties. He wrote nothing more after the age of 65, and his last years, already clouded by the death of the wife to whom he was devoted, were tormented by gout and arthritis. He died at Souvigny in January 1888.

'Marc-Michel'

Labiche's collaborator on this play was Marc Antoine Amédée Michel (1812-68). He was an old college friend of Labiche, and worked on more than 100 farces: 50 with Labiche, 48 with other collaborators, and two on his own. On the style of his work and on the nature of his collaboration with Labiche, see 'Labiche and Co' page xiii.

An Italian Straw Hat: **What Happens in the Play**

Fadinard, a wealthy Parisian bachelor, is about to marry
Hélène, daughter of a suburban market-gardener. It is
the morning of the wedding, and Hélène, her blustering
father Nonancourt and eight cabfuls of guests are expected
at any moment. Fadinard has galloped ahead to make final
arrangements. On the way he has stopped to rest his horse,
and the animal has eaten a straw hat hung on a bush while
its owner dallies in the undergrowth with a soldier. The
hat-woman and the soldier have followed Fadinard home,
and he is horrified to find that the woman is a former girlfriend (with the most jealous husband in Paris). Her soldier
lover demands a replacement hat, Fadinard rushes out to
find one – and the newly-arrived wedding-party, thinking
that he is on his way to the ceremony, jump into their cabs
and follow him.

The rest of the play is a delirious chase, faster and faster as
Fadinard hunts the hat and the guests hunt Fadinard. He goes
to a hat-shop, and finds that its owner (another former girlfriend) has sold her last Italian straw hat to the Duchess of
Champigny. (The guests mistake the hat-shop for a wedding-
parlour and the clerk, Tardiveau, for the Mayor.) Fadinard
visits the Duchess, who takes him for a tenor and hires him
to sing for her party guests – a situation he exploits by
agreeing to perform only if she hands over the Italian straw
hat. But the Duchess has given it to her god-daughter,
Madame Beauperthuis, and Fadinard once more rushes after
it. (The wedding guests, meantime, have taken the Duchess's
music-party for a reception and mingled with the aristocratic
audience, to maximum confusion.)

At Madame Beauperthuis's house, her husband is grumpily curing himself of a headache by soaking his feet in a mustard bath. His wife went out that morning to buy a pair of gloves, and hasn't come back, and he, the most jealous husband in Paris, suspects the worst. Fadinard arrives and demands a straw hat with menaces. The wedding guests swarm after him, taking Beauperthuis's house for a hotel and his bedroom for the bridal suite. Discovering to his horror that Beauperthuis's wife is his former girlfriend from the beginning of the play (the one whose hat was eaten), Fadinard rushes out, followed by the enraged Beauperthuis and the wedding party.

Late that evening, in the square outside Fadinard's house, Tardiveau (the hat-shop clerk the guests mistook for the Mayor) is on duty as a special constable. Just as everyone arrives onstage, it begins to rain. Fadinard faces harassment from the soldier for not finding the hat, trouble from Beauperthuis for seducing his wife, and fury from Nonancourt and the guests when they find out what's been happening. There is a frantic argument, drawing in not only the main characters but a neighbour woken by the noise − and it ends only when one of the wedding guests, Fadinard's deaf old uncle Vézinet, produces his present, an Italian straw hat identical to the one eaten by the horse. Fadinard hands it to the soldier's girlfriend, the tangle of cross-purposes is unravelled at last, Fadinard's wedding is saved, and the play ends in a whirl of celebration.

Vaudeville and the 'Well-Made' Play

An Italian Straw Hat takes elements from two of the most popular forms of 19th-century French theatre, vaudeville and the 'well-made' play, and marries them. Vaudeville was satirical farce, lampooning the *bourgeoisie* and using slapstick, dance, song and such stock characters as dodderer, philanderer, pretty girl, jealous husband and peppery soldier. The 'well-made' play depended on a tightly-organised plot in which the entire action was motivated by some secret involving the main character, a secret revealed only gradually as the play proceeded, until by the final curtain full knowledge had completely changed everyone's lives – for the worse in a 'well-made' melodrama, for the better in a 'well-made' farce.

In serious drama, the 'well-made' formula led to such 19th-century masterpieces as Dumas' *The Lady of the Camellias*, Ibsen's *A Doll's House* or Sardou's *Tosca* – not to mention such later examples as Rattigan's *The Winslow Boy* or the 'problem' films and TV movies based on real court cases and popular in the 1980s and 1990s. In comedy it was used in thousands of farces, most of them deservedly forgotten but including such treasures as Wilde's *The Importance of Being Earnest*, Feydeau's *A Flea in Her Ear* and Labiche's own *Célimare*. When Labiche began writing in the 1830s, dramatists were still experimenting with ways of writing 'well-made' farce, and it took him eleven years and two dozen plays to perfect and streamline the form: his *A Young Man in a Hurry* (1848) is one of the first masterworks of the genre.

An Italian Straw Hat

An Italian Straw Hat was first produced three years and 31 plays after *A Young Man in a Hurry*, at the Théâtre du Palais-Royal in Paris on April 14th, 1851. The theatre manager, Charles Dormeuil, staged it as a favour, since Labiche had already provided him with a dozen successes. But he was so unimpressed by what he called the play's 'wildness' and inconsequentiality that he arranged to be out of Paris for the first night, hoping that all would be over and forgotten by the time he returned. So far from being a flop, however, *An Italian Straw Hat* triumphed. Critics described a 'fireball of laughter' running round the theatre; several people became so helpless with mirth that they had to be revived in the foyer, and one unfortunate had a fatal stroke; instead of the usual run of some 20 performances, the piece played to full houses, in repertoire, for the next eleven months, the equivalent of a run of years today.

Most unusually for a farce, *An Italian Straw Hat* won almost immediate acclaim not only from the public, but from critics and academics alike, one even going so far as to call it 'Labiche's *Hamlet*'. It was more frequently revived than any other of Labiche's plays, and when he published his 'Complete Works' in 1878, he placed it first in the first volume. In the 80 years after its creation, it received more than 100 productions in France alone, and in 1938 it was taken into the repertoire of the Comédie-Française, where it has remained ever since: the renowned farce-actors Jacques Charon and Louis de Funès had particular success with it in the 1940s and 1950s. It was first played in English in the 1880s, and the first German translation appeared soon afterwards. Orson Welles directed a New York production in 1936 (retitled *Horse Eats Hat*, marred by over-frantic slapstick and starring, somewhat improbably in view of his later acting-style, Joseph Cotten). Comedians and actors of all kinds, from Jack Benny to Laurence Olivier, from Fernandel to Tom Conti, have played the part of Fadinard. The play had enormous influence on sketch-comedians in music-hall, for example those of Fred Karno's Circus in the 1900s. Many of them, in turn, emigrated to the US, and carried the style into early silent films: both straightforward slapstick (such as the films of the Keystone Cops) and subtler, more satirical farce (such as the films of Buster Keaton and Harold Lloyd) owe debts to its style, structure and approach. The finest silent film of the play itself was made by René Clair in 1927 – a masterpiece to which dozens of later comedian-directors acknowledged debts, including Chaplin, Stan Laurel, Tati and Jerry Lewis. In another memorable film version, made in 1941, Fernandel repeated his stage triumph: a forgotten gem. And in Britain, at least, the play has had its influence in other media: notably, on the construction of TV sitcoms, for example those of John Cleese and Connie Booth, whose character of Basil Fawlty and whose scripts for *Fawlty Towers*, with their meticulous escalations of lunacy, were the fruit of much reading of Feydeau and Labiche.

After a century and a half of such influences, it can be hard to appreciate just how original *An Italian Straw Hat* actually was, and is. Until this play, the exuberance and satirical abundance of vaudeville lacked a formal structure, and pieces were either short (like the 20-minute sketches of music-hall or pantomime) or sprawling and undisciplined. Conversely, 'well-made' farces had a strictly-organised form but nothing much to say: dullness of content is a major fault in the work even of experts like Scribe. Labiche's stroke of genius in *An Italian Straw Hat* was to marry the two styles. The play takes the form of the picaresque quest (a centuries-old standby of such 'grand' literature as the *Odyssey*, *Don Quixote* or *Tom Jones*) and spoofs it by turning up the speed, so that instead of a years-long ramble through someone's life, we have a twelve-hour gallop from breakfast to bedtime, and the object of the whole exercise is not self-discovery or full philosophical understanding, but a fancy hat with ribbons.

On to this structure Labiche grafts all the techniques of 'well-made' farce. Instead of one secret, known to the audience but only gradually revealed to the characters, there are dozens. Nothing is what the characters think it is: even the final dénouement depends on some of the people taking one Italian straw hat for another. There is plentiful *quiproquo* ('misunderstanding'), not only of words (for example when deaf old Vézinet hears one thing and thinks it means another) but of places and of people. Anaïs, who appears to be no more than a soldier's floozie, turns out first to be Fadinard's ex-girlfriend and then the wife of Beauperthuis. Clara, the hat-shop owner, is revealed as another of Fadinard's old flames, and her clerk is taken for a Mayor and later becomes a constable. Fadinard himself is mistaken for an opera-singer and a burglar. A hat-shop is a Mayor's parlour, a Duchess's villa a hotel, a *bourgeois* bedroom a bridal suite, and so on. In most 'well-made' farces there is just one *scène à faire* ('busy scene'), during which enormous confusion is gradually, painfully and hilariously untangled; in *An Italian Straw Hat* each of the five Acts builds into its own *scène à faire*.

Delirious pace is the key to the play's surface hilarity. Labiche famously described farce as 'a thousand-legged beast that must keep running, for if it slows down we yawn and if it stops we boo', and few plays better show his ability to create the 'fireball of laughter' which keeps an audience breathless. Characters incessantly snatch things from one another, bang furniture on the ground, pour hot water in other people's mustard baths, hold each other up with pistols, perform drunken dances, splash through puddles in the rain – an endless whirl of activity. But productions which turn the play into nothing more than a blur of pratfalls and manic stage-effects miss a major part of what it offers. Labiche always insisted that he was a writer of satire – this was the basis of his claim to be admitted to the Académie française – and in his finest plays the hilarity depends in part on a sustained send-up of middle-class obsessions and manners, and hints at darker themes which deepen the laughter-flow without ever impeding it (a trick later imitated by Feydeau). If *An Italian Straw Hat* had been vaudeville pure and simple, its characters would have been no more than stock braggarts, bullies and zanies, as lightly sketched as the Duchess and Achille in Act Three. But Labiche builds commentary into the characterisation, so that (for example) Nonancourt's obsession with 'doing things right' or Tardiveau's amiably fussy attention to duty become not merely personal tics but emblematic of a whole class and type of person, and the truth-to-life of even such minor characters as Beauperthuis, Albert and Vézinet bursts out of the farcical frame. And Fadinard himself is by no means the mechanistic puppet some productions make him. His panic has as much to do with personality as with the need to extricate himself from misunderstandings. In fact, given the depth of Labiche's character-drawing in other plays, it is hardly too fanciful to suggest that the hat represents married respectability, and that a confirmed bachelor and philanderer such as Fadinard is in a panic as much about finding it as not finding it.

'Labiche and Co'

After a disastrous production of *An Italian Straw Hat* in 1898, ten years after Labiche's death, the playwright Henri Becque commented with sour glee that a flop was no more than should be expected, given that Labiche's reputation had been grossly exaggerated for years. Labiche, he claimed, was not an individual writer of genius (such as, by implication, Becque was himself) but merely one member of a guild of dramatic artisans, 'Labiche and Co'. Not only that, but Labiche was the company hack: it was his collaborators who supplied all the theatrical panache and talent.

Becque's comments present an almost exact mirror-image of the truth. During the 1840s-1880s, Labiche and his collaborators were all part of the same tightly-knit group of playwrights providing stage entertainment in Paris. Collaboration was the rule rather than the exception. Labiche wrote only seven solo pieces (out of some 164); in the others, he worked with 48 different collaborators, of whom the most frequent were Marc-Michel (50 plays), Auguste Lefranc (36 plays), Alfred Delacour (25 plays) and Édouard Martin (11 plays). Each of these men, when not working with Labiche, wrote plays individually or with one another – and none has the panache of the plays they wrote with him. His 'signature' is on every line, and the only detectable differences between plays written with this collaborator or that are that his plays with Martin are particularly strong on satire and his plays with Marc-Michel (including *An Italian Straw Hat*) are frenzied romps, what the critic Jacques Robichard called 'funny nightmares'. Marc-Michel was a master of slapstick action, and specialised in 'running' plays, in which the plot was manipulated to provide as many ludicrous exits and entrances as possible. In his farces with other writers, this is the main ingredient of the humour – and without the tight plotting, good-humour and wit provided by Labiche, it is seldom enough to sustain an evening.

A glimpse of Labiche's working methods with his collaborators is provided by Émile Augier (1820-89), who wrote *The Martin*

Prize with him in 1874. As a first stage, the partners worked together on a plot-outline and a scene-by-scene synopsis. Then one of them – in *The Martin Prize*, as in *An Italian Straw Hat*, it was Labiche – wrote a complete draft script, which the other topped and tailed. Augier said that for *The Martin Prize* all he had to do was 'make a few cuts, trim a couple of exits, and that was that'. Labiche, by contrast, described his revisions of his collaborators' drafts in other plays as 'adding French polish' or 'making it funny'. When the plays reached rehearsal, further revisions were made by the writers and actors, so that the final script was the fruit of a collaborative process involving several people. But throughout the process Labiche was firmly in charge. It was he, not his collaborators, who was elected to the Académie française, and the 'Collected works' published in 1878-9 are remembered as his, not theirs. If 'Labiche and Co' ever existed, he was less its journeyman than its master-craftsman.

Music

A main ingredient of *An Italian Straw Hat*, often ignored today, is the 25 short songs (a remnant of the vaudeville tradition) which stud the action. Except for the finales to Acts Three and Five, they are not so much full-blown music numbers as short, doggerel inserts lasting no more than a few seconds each. In Labiche's time they were sung to snippets and snatches of well-known tunes, many of which have since been lost.

Labiche (who was tone-deaf) regularly complained about having to put music in his plays, and from the mid-1850s onwards developed a kind of farce which dispensed with songs. In some of his early plays, the songs are pointless interruptions,

destroying the comic rhythm – for example when two partners
in a domestic row suddenly burst into ten lines of Christmas-
cardish verse. But in several plays, notably those written with
Marc-Michel, the music helps to create an atmosphere of
surrealism, irony and saturnalia which is vital to the action.
One critic (Jean-Jacques Weiss) went so far as to compare the
music of *An Italian Straw Hat*, and particularly the numbers
involving the wedding guests, to the choruses of Greek drama:
establishing mood, shaping and controlling the dramatic flow.

Music numbers fulfil a second important function. In all farce,
a great part of the spectators' pleasure comes from constant
awareness that what they are seeing is a piece of technical
bravura. When we watch tragedy, we are drawn into the action
to the point where, ideally, the identities of actor and character
merge and become indistinguishable. In comedy, by contrast,
the performers' personalities and performing-skills are always
with us, and our pleasure depends partly on constant awareness, constant reminders, that what we are seeing is a show
and that the skills of the performers are being deployed precisely to delight us. If Hamlet or Lear started to tap-dance, sing
doggerel or perform slapstick, the effect would be quite different
from the same routines in a farce performance. The music in
An Italian Straw Hat keeps breaking the illusion of reality, drawing us across the footlights and making us accomplices not just
in the action but in the performance of that action.

Down the years, some productions have neglected this aspect
of the play. Even Labiche himself authorised productions
without songs – and however exhilarating and satisfying, they
are substantially different from his original intentions. The
present edition allows for both kinds of experience. The text is
printed as straightforward farce without the music numbers,

but the music cues are indicated and their words are supplied in the Appendix, page 91.

The Original Production

The Théâtre du Palais-Royal, for which Labiche wrote *An Italian Straw Hat*, employed him practically as house dramatist, and he wrote 97 plays for it over 40 years. He was one of a dozen writers supplying materials, and their plays and sketches were performed in repertory, appearances being curtailed or increased according to demand. (The shortest Labiche 'run' was three-quarters of an hour, the play being cancelled half-way through the first performance. The longest was *An Italian Straw Hat*, which stayed in the repertory for eleven months, and was constantly revived.)

The figure of 97 plays surprises those commentators who think of Labiche and his fellow-writers as 'literary' dramatists in the manner of, say, Beaumarchais. In fact the playwrights were more like the authors of today's TV sitcoms, producing work which was never intended to be anything but ephemeral. Usually Labiche took an idea to the theatre manager, was given a commission (sometimes for as much as three years ahead) and then selected a collaborator and wrote the play. But the initial idea could also come from the other side. In June 1854, for example, the manager of the Palais-Royal wrote saying that he'd hired a troupe of Spanish dancers for the summer, and needed a play to put them in – 'two acts, with a dance sequence to end each half. Doesn't matter what it's about, but make it funny.'

Another similarity with sitcoms is that each theatre in Labiche's 'circuit' had its own resident company of actors, and the plays were tailored to fit their skills. The Palais-Royal company stayed largely unchanged for thirty years (throughout Labiche's most fertile period), and included some of the leading farceurs in Paris: Ravel who excelled at harassed parts and had a pleasant singing voice (he played Fadinard in *An Italian Straw Hat*), Amant who played dodderers (in this play, Vézinet), Lhéritier and Valaire who specialised in outrage and bluster (they played, respectively, Beauperthuis and Émile), Chauvière who played dumb blondes (Hélène) and Azimont who played vivacious young flirts (Clara) and was renowned for her low-cut costumes.

The Palais-Royal was a whole area as well as a theatre. Originally the palace and gardens of Cardinal Richelieu, the minister of Louis XIV, at the time of the Revolution it was opened to the public as a vast pleasure-garden, complete with walks, bandstands, restaurants, bars and a dozen places of entertainment ranging from dance-rooms and music-halls to the Comédie-Française (built on the site of Richelieu's original private theatre, where Molière had been resident dramatist). Before the Théâtre du Palais-Royal itself began to specialise in farce, it had housed straight plays, puppet-shows, mimes and circus acts, including, at one stage, a troupe of performing dogs. Its great days of farce continued after Labiche's death: Feydeau's most elaborate plays were first staged there.

The Palais-Royal was a medium-sized theatre, seating some 800 spectators in a pit, boxes and galleries. The proscenium stage, originally lit by candles, was converted to gas lighting in Labiche's time: the street-lamp in Act Five of *An Italian Straw Hat* was no mere plot-contrivance, but a novelty in its own right. Furniture and costumes were as elaborate as budgets would allow – as Labiche once wrote, 'People go to the theatre for beauty and extravagance. Drabness and propriety they can get at home.' Sets – called 'box sets' because they were like boxes with the side facing the spectators cut away – were painted on canvas scenery-flats, were often decorated with real flowers and plants, and were changed during the act-breaks while pit musicians played entr'actes. Plays like *An Italian Straw Hat*, in five acts and filling an entire evening, were rare. The usual bill consisted of two, three or more unrelated pieces: a two-act farce, say, a couple of one-acters and a monologue. These components could be changed from evening to evening, so that the bills were never the same two nights running – a fact which both explains the theatre's gluttony for material, and makes even more remarkable the long run of *An Italian Straw Hat* (too elaborate to share a bill with any other show.)

Because all those involved knew each other well, and because the parts in each play were tailored for specific performers, there was no such person as a director. The stage manager organised rehearsals, and the theatre manager and author took part throughout. As soon as moves and business were established, they were written down in the prompt-book, which became the production 'Bible'. (Feydeau often published his plays from these prompt-books, and details of moves and business can take up to one third of the total text. Labiche, by contrast, published his original texts, and his stage-directions are sparse.) Apparently some actors developed cherished pieces of business, using them in play after play – and if the script failed to give an opportunity, they made one. The audience was fairly constant – some patrons of the Palais-Royal went so regularly that the actors directed asides to them specifically, by name – and there was more by-play between stage and auditorium than we favour today. In one Labiche farce, the words *Embrassons-nous, Folleville* ('Kiss me, Folleville') became an instant catchphrase, and just before the actor used it he cued the entire audience, who roared it out in unison – by no means the kind of effect favoured at the Comédie-Française across the road.

Kenneth McLeish, 1996

For Further Reading

Although for French-speakers there exist an excellent edition of 42 plays (edited by Jacques Robichez and published by Robert Laffont in 1991) and a fine critical biography (Philippe Soupault, *Eugène Labiche*, 1964), books in English are few and far between. Leonard C. Pronko, *Eugène Labiche and Georges Feydeau* (1982) is an enthusiastic introduction, and Marvin Carlson, *The French Stage in the Nineteenth Century* (1972) meticulously sets the context. Jessica M. Davis, *Farce* (1978) is an excellent survey of the genre. Otherwise, information and comment are scattered in learned journals and the introductions to this or that translation. Readers with access to university libraries are recommended to Émile Augier's Introduction to Labiche's *Complete Plays* of 1878 (translated in the Winter 1959 issue of Tulane Drama Review) and to Eric Bentley's much-reprinted essay on 'The Psychology of Farce' (originally published in R.H. Ward's 1958 volume of plays in translation, Sardou's *Let's Get a Divorce and Other Plays*). The rest (so far) is a deafening silence.

Labiche: Key Dates

1815   Born.

1834   Having passed his *baccalauréat*, goes with friends on an extended trip abroad; later writes it up in a new magazine (*Chérubin*) he and they have founded. Begins (reluctantly) to study law.

1835   Begins writing theatre reviews.

1837   With friends, writes a collaborative novel and his first-ever farce, *The Washstand Basin*.

1838-48   Writes 24 plays, marries, travels throughout Europe.

1848   First venture into politics.

1848-51   Writes a play a month.

1851   *An Italian Straw Hat.*

1853   First of many declarations that he is tired both of Paris and of farce; buys a farm at Souvigny, writing of it 'Here I am in paradise'.

1853-63   Writes 58 plays.

1863   *Moi* accepted by the Comédie-Française, an honour for which Labiche has worked for three years.

1868   Elected Mayor of Souvigny (a post he was to hold for the next eight years).

1869   Onset of rheumatoid arthritis, which he combats by taking cures abroad and by extensive hunting at Souvigny.

1876   Health stops responding to these treatments.

1878   *Complete Plays* begin to appear.

1879   Last play (*Embrassons-nous, Folleville*) performed; publication completed of first ten volumes of *Complete Plays*; health problems increase.

1880   Elected to the Académie française.

1888   After eight years of increasing ill health (chronic arthritis, gout, liver and kidney problems), dies.

AN ITALIAN STRAW HAT

Characters

Act One:

FADINARD, *a man of means*
FÉLIX, *his servant*
VIRGINIE, *a maidservant*
VÉZINET, *a deaf old man*
ÉMILE, *an army officer*
ANAÏS, *his lover*
NONANCOURT,
    a nurseryman
HÉLÈNE, *the bride, his
    daughter*
BOBIN, *his nephew*

Act Two:

CLARA, *owner of a hat-shop*
TARDIVEAU, *a book-keeper*

Act Three:

DUCHESS OF
    CHAMPIGNY
ACHILLE DE ROSALBA
BUTLER
MAID

Act Four:

BEAUPERTHUIS,
    a bad-tempered man

Act Five:

TROUILLEBERT,
    a special constable
CROSS MAN

Wedding guests; guests in Act Three; constables; citizens.

The action takes place in Paris, in the mid-19th century.

*Note: music cues are indicated by numbers in the play-text.
For the lyrics, see Appendix, page 91.*

ACT ONE

FADINARD*'s drawing-room. Main double door, centre. Subsidiary doors, left and right. Enter* VIRGINIE *and* FÉLIX. FÉLIX *is trying to kiss her.*

VIRGINIE. No, Félix. I haven't time.

FÉLIX. Just one kiss.

VIRGINIE. Not now.

FÉLIX. We come from the same village.

VIRGINIE. I've to kiss everyone who comes from our village?

FÉLIX. It's not all that big . . .

VIRGINIE. You told me your boss was getting married this morning. Monsieur Fadinard. 'Come and see the presents,' you said. Well, show me the presents.

FÉLIX. There's no hurry. His Nibs went out of town yesterday. To his pa-in-law's. To sign some document. He won't be here till eleven o'clock. They'll all be here. To go to the Town Hall.

VIRGINIE. What's the bride like?

FÉLIX. Nothing to write home about. But quite a catch. Her father's a market gardener. Nonancourt.

VIRGINIE. Félix . . . if she's looking for a maid, a personal maid . . . mention my name.

FÉLIX. You don't like it where you are? Working for Monsieur Beauperthuis?

VIRGINIE. Monsieur Beauperthuis. That crab, that weasel, that . . . warthog. Not to mention his wife. She's a . . . No, I mustn't.

FÉLIX. Quite right.

VIRGINIE. She's a . . . She's always on the . . . Always got a . . .

FÉLIX. She hasn't.

VIRGINIE. She has. Every time Monsieur Beauperthuis goes out – *poof!* She's off as well. And where to? Who with? You may well ask.

FÉLIX. You can't possibly stay on in a house like that.

VIRGINIE (*shyly*). Besides, it would be nice to work in the same house as someone else from our village.

FÉLIX (*taking her in his arms*). Same county, anyway.

Enter VÉZINET, *carrying a wedding present.*

VÉZINET. It's all right, it's only me. Uncle Vézinet. Have we started?

FÉLIX (*smiling at him*). Not yet, grandad.

VIRGINIE. Félix!

FÉLIX. It's all right. He's as deaf as a post. Watch. (*To* VÉZINET, *in baby talk.*) Going to the wedding, then, are we? Going to enjoy ourselves? Won't that be nice? (*Offering him a seat.*) Time for beddy-byes.

VÉZINET. Just what I always say. I thought at first we were meeting at the Town Hall, so I went to the Town Hall. They said we were meeting here, so I came here.

FÉLIX. Well, it is Thursday.

VÉZINET. Not now, thanks. I went before I came. (*To* VIRGINIE.) Put this with the others, would you, my dear? Careful. It's fragile.

VIRGINIE (*aside*). I'll have a good look while I'm in there. (*Sweetly to him.*) Bye-bye, sweetie-pie.

Exit right.

VÉZINET. What a charming child. Heh, heh, if I was five years younger . . .

FÉLIX (*smiling*). Dirty old man. You're past it, grandad.

VÉZINET. Just what I always say. (*Aside.*) What a bright young man.

Enter FADINARD, *talking to someone offstage.*

FADINARD. Unharness him and rub him down, would you? (*Onstage.*) What a business! Cost me two francs, but it was worth every penny. Ah, Félix.

FÉLIX. Monsieur Fadinard.

FADINARD. You'll never believe this, but –

FÉLIX. Where's everyone else, Monsieur? The wedding party?

FADINARD. Still in Charentonneau, getting into their cabs. Eight cabs. I hurried on ahead, to see that everything's in order. Are all the presents here?

FÉLIX. Yes, Monsieur. (*Pointing right.*) In there.

FADINARD. Splendid. You'll never believe this, but when I left Charentonneau, at eight this morning . . .

VÉZINET (*aside*). That's my nephew. He never notices *anything*.

FADINARD. Uncle Vézinet! (*To* FÉLIX.) You go. I'll tell him instead. (*To* VÉZINET, *as* FÉLIX *goes*.) You'll never believe this, but when I left Charentonneau, at eight this morning . . .

VÉZINET. Not now, thanks. And where's the blushing bride?

FADINARD. She's on her way. In eight cabs.

He tries again.

You'll never believe this, but -

VÉZINET (*shaking his hand*). Well, my dear boy, congratulations.

FADINARD. Uncle . . . (*Continuing.*) What I was saying, I was in my pony-trap, coming along the road from Charentonneau, when I realised I'd dropped my whip.

VÉZINET. You're a credit to the family.

FADINARD. Pardon? Ah. (*Continuing.*) It's got a silver handle. I shouted 'Whoa.' I stopped. I got out. I looked. A hundred yards up the road, I found it. In a bramble patch. Nearly scratched myself to death.

VÉZINET. Just what I always say. 'He's bound to go far. You mark my − '

FADINARD. And *then*, when I got back to the trap, it'd gone. No trap, no horse.

FÉLIX (*at the door*). Mislaid your horse, Monsieur?

FADINARD. Félix. I'm talking to my uncle. Family business. Private.

VÉZINET. Not now, thanks. Mind you, good husbands make good wives.

FADINARD. Yes. Bibble, bibble, bibble. Anyway, trap gone. Horse gone. What to do? Investigate. Question witnesses. 'There's a trap over there, beside the wood.' There was. Mine. Not to mention the horse. Chewing a bunch of straw, with poppies. Next minute, a woman's voice. 'My hat! My hat!' Not a bunch of straw, not a horse's lunch, a hat. She'd hung it on a bush while she talked to a soldier.

FÉLIX (*aside*). As you do.

FADINARD (*to* VÉZINET). I say *talked*, but you know what I really think.

VÉZINET. The big house on the corner.

FADINARD. Bibble, bibble.

VÉZINET. Beside the fire station.

FADINARD. Just what I always say. I was just about to apologise, when her soldier stormed up. Proper little Napoleon. 'I say, you there, chappie . . . ' − that kind of thing. 'Are you addressing me?' I said. 'I most certainly am,' he said. 'I see,' I said. So he charged. I jumped. Next thing I'm in the trap, the horse bolts, and here I am. Oh, I *did* throw him five francs for the hat. Or was it ten centimes? I'll check later. I hadn't time to look.

He takes out a piece of straw hat, with poppies.

This is all that was left.

VÉZINET (*turning it over*). Nice piece of straw.

FADINARD. At that price, it would be.

VÉZINET. You won't find another one like it. I know.

FÉLIX. Let's have a look.

FADINARD. Félix! This is a private hat.

FÉLIX. Oh, sorry I'm sure. Excuse me. I'll go where I'm appreciated.

He stays.

VÉZINET. Tell me, what time are we meeting at the Town Hall?

FADINARD. Eleven o'clock. E-le-ven o'clock.

He holds up eleven fingers.

VÉZINET. Lunch will be late. I think I'll make a cup of tea. Excuse me . . .

False exit.

FADINARD. Glad to.

VÉZINET (*coming back, hand outstretched*). A credit. A credit.

FADINARD. What? Oh. Thanks. (*Aside, as he shakes hands.*) As soon as I'm married, out he goes.

VÉZINET. Not now, thanks. But it was nice of you to ask.

FADINARD. Thankyou, Uncle. [MUSIC 1]

Exeunt VÉZINET *and* FÉLIX *left, with the piece of hat.*

FADINARD. At last! In an hour's time, I'll be married. That fool Nonancourt won't be shouting 'It's all off!' every five minutes. The man's a pig. A warthog. I met him on a bus. He was kicking my shin. I was just going to thump him, when I saw his daughter. Opened my fist. Passed his fare along to the conductor. After that, it was no time before we were like *that*, the two of us. Nurseryman . . . Charentonneau . . . Love makes us bold. I said, 'You couldn't let me have a packet of carrot seeds?' He said, 'No, but I've got some fine geraniums.' It was a green light, that answer. 'How much?' 'One franc the pot.' 'I'll have one!' We get to his place . . . I buy four pots (it was Félix's birthday) . . . I ask for his daughter's hand. 'But what do you do?' 'Do? I'm a gentleman.' 'Well off?' 'Yes, thankyou.' 'How well?' 'Fifty francs.' 'Out!' 'Per day.' 'Stay!' Oh, you *can* picture it? Next thing I know, I'm supping on sauerkraut with Bobin. Bobin, the cousin. Bobin the booby. Keeps shaking hands, kissing my fiancée. 'There's no harm in it,' people say. 'They were children together.' That's another thing that's got to stop. As soon as I'm married, I'll . . . Brrr! I'm sorry. It's just that word. After all these years as a bachelor . . . Oh, you, too? Well, there you are, then. In an hour I'll be . . . (*Quickly.*) married. Love, honour, all that. And kissing. Without that warthog shouting 'Son-in-law, keep off the grass!' You'll like Hélène. Wait till you see her in her wedding dress.

[MUSIC 2]

A rose, a posy of roses. Ahh, I've booked such a pretty room. Rosewood panelling, yellow velvet curtains. The honeymoon suite. I just can't wait.

Noises, off.

They're here. Her, here. The guests. I'll never get used to this.

Enter ANAÏS, *trying to restrain* ÉMILE. *She is hatless; he is in uniform.*

ANAÏS. No, Émile. Please.

ÉMILE. Steady. Calm nerves. Whoa, now.

FADINARD (*aside*). The lady with the hat. And her Napoleon. Now what?

ANAÏS. Please don't make a scene.

ÉMILE. Leave this to me, I said. (*To* FADINARD.) Ha-HA! Didn't expect to see us so soon, did you?

FADINARD. My dear chap . . . Madame . . . How kind of you to call. The thing is, this morning it's rather . . . I'm rather . . . (*Aside.*) What do they *want*?

ÉMILE. Well? Lady present. Offer seat, why don't you?

FADINARD. Oh, I'm sorry. Do sit down, Madame. My manners . . . (*Aside as* ANAÏS *sits.*) My wedding guests!

ÉMILE. Fine horse. Yours. Fine.

FADINARD. How kind. You . . . er . . . *walked?*

ÉMILE. Of course we didn't walk. What d'you take us for, man?

FADINARD. Oh, er, ah. (*Aside.*) Napoleon!

ANAÏS. Émile, it's time we . . . we really ought to be . . .

FADINARD. That's right. You really ought to be . . . (*Aside.*) They'll be here any moment.

ÉMILE. Monsieur, seems to me, what you need, lesson or two in politeness.

FADINARD. How dare you? I was top in that in school.

ÉMILE. This morning, you left . . . abruptly.

FADINARD. The horse was in a hurry.

ÉMILE. And you dropped this coin. Accidentally, I'm sure.

FADINARD (*aside*). Ten centimes. It was ten centimes. (*Aloud.*) I'm so sorry. It just slipped out. So kind of you to call. Here you are.

ÉMILE. What's that?

FADINARD. Five francs. For the hat.

ÉMILE. Monsieur!

ANAÏS. Émile!

ÉMILE. Sorry. Keep one's cool. Did promise.

FADINARD (*rummaging in his purse*). I'm terribly sorry. Wasn't that enough? I've only got small change.

ÉMILE. Nothing to do with change. Not here for change.

FADINARD. Oh, not? Well, if not, what?

ÉMILE. Apology. Down on knees, apologise.

FADINARD. Who, me?

ANAÏS. There's no need. Really.

ÉMILE (*aside to her*). Leave this to *me*.

FADINARD. It's hardly my fault. I didn't eat your hat in person. And then my horse . . . he'd a perfect right . . .

ÉMILE. Monsieur?

FADINARD. We have to ask ourselves: why did Madame hang her hat where she hung it? A bush isn't a hatstand. What was she doing there anyway? Woods, soldiers . . . these questions must be asked.

ANAÏS. Monsieur!

ÉMILE. Are you suggesting – ?

ANAÏS. Monsieur Tavernier!

FADINARD. Tavernier? Who's Tavernier?

ÉMILE. I am.

ANAÏS. He's my cousin. We were children together.

FADINARD (*aside*). They all say that.

ANAÏS. I was in the wood with him to . . . talk to him . . . discuss his career . . . to stiffen his morale . . .

FADINARD. Without a hat?

ÉMILE. Monsieur!

He picks up a chair and crashes it down again.

ANAÏS. Émile!

ÉMILE. Leave this to *me*!

FADINARD. Who said you could smash my furniture? I'll throw you . . . (*Aside.*) No I won't. He might land on the wedding guests.

ÉMILE. Not another word, Monsieur.

FADINARD. Oh, good.

HUBERT. Down on knees, apologise – or not?

FADINARD. Oh, for Heaven's sake. (*On his knees.*) Madame, I beg you, in all humility, please, I . . . oh, for Heaven's sake, I won't do it again.

He gets up.

ÉMILE. Not enough.

FADINARD. It's all you're getting.

ÉMILE (*smashing another chair*). Monsieur!

FADINARD. Stop doing that.

ÉMILE. I've hardly started.

NONANCOURT (*off*). Son-in-law! Son-in-law!

ANAÏS. Someone's coming.

FADINARD (*aside*). It's them. Now what?

ANAÏS. Where can I hide? Ah!

She runs to the door left. FADINARD *runs after her.*

FADINARD. You can't go in there – (*To* ÉMILE.) General . . .

ÉMILE. Get rid of these people. Then, we'll talk.

Exeunt ÉMILE *and* ANAÏS. FADINARD *shuts the door on them just in time. Enter, from the other door,* NONANCOURT, BOBIN *and* HÉLÈNE *in her wedding dress.*

FADINARD. Phew!

NONANCOURT. It's all off, son-in-law. You've got no idea. No manners, no idea.

HÉLÈNE. Papa.

NONANCOURT. Quiet, Hélène.

FADINARD. But what have I done?

NONANCOURT. There's a whole wedding party down those stairs, outside. Eight cabs.

BOBIN. Magnificent.

FADINARD. What about it?

NONANCOURT. You were not at the door to greet us.

BOBIN. To shake our hands.

NONANCOURT. Apologise to my daughter.

HÉLÈNE. Papa.

NONANCOURT. Quiet, Hélène. (*To* FADINARD.) Apologise.

FADINARD. Oh, for Heaven's sake. (*On his knees.*) My dear, I beg you, in all humility, please, I . . . oh, for Heaven's sake, I won't do it again.

NONANCOURT. And another thing. Why did you gallop off this morning without so much as saying 'Ta-ta'?

BOBIN. Or shaking hands.

NONANCOURT. Quiet, Bobin. (*To* FADINARD.) Well?

FADINARD. You were all asleep.

BOBIN. Not true. *I* was polishing my boots.

NONANCOURT. I know we're plain folk. Nothing fancy, nothing lah-dee-dah −

BOBIN. That's how it is, in gardening.

NONANCOURT. − but that's no reason for bad manners.

FADINARD (*aside*). This, from *him*?

NONANCOURT. No reason for getting high and mighty.

FADINARD. Look, father-in-law, calm down. Take some liver salts.

NONANCOURT. You're not married yet, my lad. I can still break the whole thing off.

BOBIN. Break it off. Ooh, yes.

NONANCOURT. You'll tread on my toes just once too often.

He gives his foot a violent wriggle.

Ee-ow-ouch.

FADINARD. Now what?

NONANCOURT. These lah-dee-dah shoes. They're killing me. Ee-ow-ouch.

HÉLÈNE. Walk up and down, Papa. You'll break them in.

Suddenly she too starts to twist and writhe.

FADINARD. They're all at it.

NONANCOURT. Have they brought that plant?

FADINARD. What plant?

NONANCOURT. It's symbolic.

FADINARD. What of?

NONANCOURT. Hey. Don't you get high and mighty again.
We're plain folk, nothing lah-dee-dah –

BOBIN. That's how it is in gardening.

FADINARD. Don't start again.

NONANCOURT. But we know what's what. That plant – I
intend to put it personally in my daughter's bedroom, so
that after she's married she can look at it any time she
likes, and say . . . (*Wriggling his foot.*) Ee-ow-ouch.

HÉLÈNE. Papa.

She, too, writhes as before.

FADINARD (*aside*). It's an epidemic.

HÉLÈNE. Papa . . .

NONANCOURT. What is it now?

HÉLÈNE. There's a pin sticking into me, round the back.

BOBIN (*rolling up his sleeves*). I'll get it.

FADINARD. Oh, no you won't.

NONANCOURT. Nay, nay, they were children together.

BOBIN. She *is* my cousin.

FADINARD. Keep off the grass!

NONANCOURT (*pointing to the door left*). Go in there.

FADINARD. No, no, no, no. Not in there.

NONANCOURT. Why not?

FADINARD. Plumbers. I've got the plumbers.

NONANCOURT (*To* HÉLÈNE). All right, walk about. Jiggle yourself. That'll shake it loose. (*Wriggling his foot.*) It's no good, I'll have to take these off.

He goes towards the door, right.

FADINARD. Not in there.

NONANCOURT. Why not?

FADINARD. I've got the chimney-sweep.

NONANCOURT. Plumbers, chimney-sweeps . . . you're a one-man employment agency. Well, they'll all be waiting outside. I'll change in the cab. Bobin, take your cousin's arm. To the Town Hall. Onward! (*Wriggling his foot.*) Ee-ow-ouch!

FADINARD. That's right. You go on. I need to get my hat.

He hustles them out.   [MUSIC 3]

As soon as they're gone, he goes to open the door, left.

Come on, Madame. You can't stay there forever. Lieutenant, *now* . . .

Without waiting for them, he goes upstage to check that NONAN-COURT *and the others are well clear.* ANAÏS *and* ÉMILE *are about to enter, when* VIRGINIE *enters from the door right, holding the piece of hat and giggling.* FADINARD *doesn't see her, and she doesn't see* ÉMILE *and* ANAÏS. *But they see her.*

ÉMILE. My God!

ANAÏS. My maid!

They hide from her.

VIRGINIE. She's in the woods, her hat's on the bushes, and then it's in the horse . . .

FADINARD (*turning sharply; aside*). Where did she come from?

VIRGINIE. It's just like Madame Anaïs'. No-o-o-o-o . . .

ÉMILE (*aside to* FADINARD). Psst. Get rid of her. Or else.

VIRGINIE. I'll have a look.

FADINARD. Oh, no you won't.

He rushes at VIRGINIE, *and snatches the piece of hat.*

Out! Shoo!

VIRGINIE. But Monsieur . . .

FADINARD. Or else, or else, or else!

VIRGINIE. Aah!

Exit, screaming. FADINARD *comes downstage.*

FADINARD. Who was that? What's happening?

ANAÏS *totters in, and collapses in his arms.*

Now she's not feeling well.

He sits her on a chair. ÉMILE *hurries to her side.*

ÉMILE. Anaïs!

FADINARD. Do cut it short. They're waiting.

NONANCOURT (*off*). Son-in-law! Son-in-law!

FADINARD. See?

ÉMILE. Sugar-water, you fool. A glass of sugar-water. Now.

FADINARD (*beside himself*). Of course! Sugar-water!

He goes to the sideboard and starts pouring and stirring sugar-water.

ÉMILE. Anaïs, light of my life . . . (*To* FADINARD.) Jump to it, man!

FADINARD (*stirring madly*). It's all stuck to the bottom. Madame, I don't want to seem rude, but I'm sure if you went home . . .

ÉMILE. Out of the question.

FADINARD. What question?

ANAÏS (*weakly*). That maid . . .

FADINARD. What about her?

ANAÏS. That was *my* maid. She recognised the hat. She'll tell my husband.

FADINARD. Good heavens, there's a husband.

ÉMILE. Of course there's a husband.

ANAÏS. And if I go home without the hat . . . He always thinks the worst. He might jump to conclusions.

FADINARD. Oh, might he?

ANAÏS. I'm ruined. I might as well be dead.

FADINARD. But not here, Madame. It's unhealthy enough already.

NONANCOURT (*off*). Son-in-law! Son-in-law!

FADINARD. See?

Absent-mindedly he drinks the sugar-water, and then goes to ÉMILE.

What are we going to do?

ÉMILE. Simple. Another hat. Exactly same. Pass it off. No problem.

FADINARD. You *are* Napoleon. (*To* ANAÏS.) Here's what's left, Madame. If you go round the shops . . .

ANAÏS. I can't do that.

ÉMILE. She can't do that.

FADINARD. She can't do that. Why can't she?

ÉMILE. Look at her. The state she's in. Where's that sugar-water?

FADINARD. Here. Good lord, someone's drunk it. (*Giving him the piece of hat.*) Look, you take this. *You're* not in a state.

ÉMILE. I can't leave her like this.

NONANCOURT (*off*). Son-in-law! Son-in-law!

FADINARD. Well, surely there's someone.

ÉMILE. Exactly. Off you go.

FADINARD. Me?

ANAÏS (*feebly*). Oh please . . . quickly . . .

FADINARD. I'm in the middle of getting married. My guests are waiting outside.

ÉMILE. So, let 'em.

FADINARD. Lieutenant!

ANAÏS. Make sure and get one exactly the same. My husband knows this one extremely well.

FADINARD. But I –

ÉMILE. With poppies on it.

FADINARD. I really don't –

ÉMILE. We'll wait till you get back. A fortnight. A month, if necessary.

FADINARD. But what about my wedding guests?

ÉMILE (*picking up a chair*). Are you going, or aren't you?

FADINARD (*snatching it*). I'm going. Leave my furniture alone. Don't touch anything. Good grief! (*Aside.*) I'll go to the nearest hat-shop. But what about the wedding guests? Eight cabs. Not to mention the Mayor.

He sits automatically on the chair he's been holding.

NONANCOURT (*off*). Son-in-law! Son-in-law!

FADINARD. I'll explain to father-in-law.

ÉMILE. Oh, no you won't. Or else.

FADINARD. Or else again! thanks very much.

NONANCOURT (*off, hammering at the door*). Son-in-law! Son-in-law!

ÉMILE. Don't let him in.

He and ANAÏS *go left and right of the double door, so that when it opens it hides them. Enter* NONANCOURT, *carrying a large potted plant.*

NONANCOURT. Son-in-law, it's all off.

FADINARD (*stopping him coming in*). That's right. Let's be off.

NONANCOURT. I'll just put this down.

FADINARD. Not here. Not here.

NONANCOURT. Whyever not?

FADINARD. Window-cleaners. Come on! Come *on*!

He hustles him out. ÉMILE *and* ANAÏS *come out.*

ANAÏS. Oh, Émile!

ÉMILE. Oh, Anaïs!

They rush into one another's arms. Enter FÉLIX.

FÉLIX. Oh, crikey!

End of Act One.

ACT TWO

A hat shop. On the counter, a large ledger. There is just one tailor's dummy with a hat on it, otherwise the shop is empty apart from seats and the counter. Enter CLARA, *talking to the shop-girls in the workshop offstage.*

CLARA. Be quick now, girls. That order's urgent. (*Onstage.*) Where on Earth is Tardiveau? He really is past it. I'll have to get someone younger.

Enter TARDIVEAU, *in formal morning dress.*

TARDIVEAU. Phew. Made it. Golly, it's hot.

He takes a handkerchief from his hat and mops his brow.

CLARA. Well done, Monsieur Tardiveau. First here, as usual.

TARDIVEAU. I'm sorry, Mamzelle Clara. I've had such a lot to do. I got up at six . . . (*Aside.*) Golly, it's hot! (*Aloud.*) . . . I lit the fire, shaved, made my dandelion tea . . .

CLARA. Why dandelion?

TARDIVEAU. Coffee's too stimulating. I mustn't be stimulated. Not in my job.

CLARA. Hat-shop clerk?

TARDIVEAU. Special Constable.

CLARA. You?

TARDIVEAU. That's right. You won't have seen my uniform. We don't wear uniform in shops.

CLARA. Monsieur Tardiveau, you're fifty-five.

TARDIVEAU (*bowing gallantly*). I'm sixty-two, Mamzelle, and at your service . . . ooh!

He straightens up with difficulty.

CLARA (*aside*). Thanks.

TARDIVEAU. I persuaded them to keep me on.

CLARA. For devotion?

TARDIVEAU. For Trouillebert.

CLARA. Trouillebert?

TARDIVEAU. Trouillebert. Clarinet teacher. We volunteer for shifts together, and spend the night playing for sugar-water. It's my one weakness. Beer just won't stay down.

He goes behind the counter.

CLARA (*aside*). He'll have to go.

TARDIVEAU (*aside*). Golly, it's hot.

CLARA. Monsieur Tardiveau, I want you to run an errand.

TARDIVEAU. Ah. D'you mind if I put on a cotton jacket first? This suit's so hot.

CLARA. Change when you get back. Go to the draper's and get me some coloured ribbons. Red, white and blue.

TARDIVEAU. Red, white and blue?

CLARA. There's a funeral next week.

TARDIVEAU. As soon as I've changed . . .

CLARA. Now.

TARDIVEAU. Yes, Mamzelle. (*Aside.*) But as soon as I get back, I'll change.

Exit.

CLARA. Well, things are looking up! Four months, plenty of orders, business flourishing. That's what happens when you put work first. Work first, not men. You can't run a business if you're running after men.

A carriage draws up outside.

A customer.

Enter FADINARD, *fast.*

FADINARD. Mamzelle, a straw hat please, immediately, right now, at once.

CLARA. A straw hat . . . (*Recognising him.*) You!

FADINARD (*aside*). Blast! Clara! What a time to meet her again. The wedding guests . . . (*Aloud, making for the door.*) None in stock, eh? I'll try later . . .

CLARA. I thought you'd never get here. Where have you been?

FADINARD. Shh! Versailles. I've just got back.

CLARA. Six months later?

FADINARD. I missed the bus. (*Aside.*) Why did it have to be *her*?

CLARA. I suppose you treat all your girls like this.

FADINARD. Shh! What? Oh. You're right to be cross.

CLARA. Right? To be cross? You said, 'We'll go for a stroll.' It began to rain. I thought you'd call a cab. But instead, you parked me under a tree –

FADINARD (*aside*). Unforgiveable.

CLARA. 'Wait here,' you said. 'I'll fetch an umbrella.' So I waited, and here you are, six months later, without the umbrella.

FADINARD. I knew I'd forgotten something. I'll just go and –

CLARA. Oh, no. First, an explanation.

FADINARD (*aside*). Eight cabs. Paid by the hour. (*Aloud.*) Clara, darling . . .

He tries to kiss her, but she pulls away.

CLARA. You said you'd marry me.

FADINARD (*aside*). I *did*? (*Aloud.*) I do, I do.

CLARA. If I catch you with anyone else, I'll make such a scene . . .

FADINARD. Someone else? Me? Someone else? You're joking. (*Change of tone.*) And that reminds me: I need an Italian straw hat immediately. With poppies.

CLARA. Aha! There *is* someone else.

FADINARD. Of course there's someone else. Guards officer. Carrying on with his Colonel's wife.

CLARA. I'll believe you. On one condition.

FADINARD. Just hurry.

CLARA. Take me out, tonight.

FADINARD. What?

CLARA. Take me to the theatre.

FADINARD. Oh, brilliant. I've been wondering what to do tonight. 'My God,' I said to myself only just now, 'What *shall* I do tonight?' Show me some hats.

CLARA. Come through to the back room. And don't make eyes at my shop-girls.

She goes into the back room. Before FADINARD *can follow,* NONANCOURT *comes in, still carrying his potted palm.*

NONANCOURT. Son-in-law, it's all off.

FADINARD. Not you as well.

NONANCOURT. Funny-looking Town Hall. Where's his Worship?

FADINARD. Won't be long. I'll fetch him. Stay where you are.

He hurries after CLARA. NONANCOURT *goes to the shop door and beckons.*   [MUSIC 4]

Enter HÉLÈNE, BOBIN, VÉZINET *and* WEDDING-GUESTS.

NONANCOURT. That's right. This is the place. The Town Hall. The wedding room. I know it's not like at home. This is Paris. Mind your manners. Keep your gloves on. (*Wriggling his foot.*) Ee-ow-ouch. These shoes are killing me. I'm weak with emotion. Weak. Hélène, my dear –

HÉLÈNE. Papa, it's still sticking into me.

NONANCOURT. Walk up and down. Jiggle a bit.

BOBIN. Uncle Nonancourt, put down your potted palm.

NONANCOURT. Nay, nay, I'll not be parted. It's for Hélène.

[MUSIC 5]

(*Wriggling his foot.*) Ee-ow-ouch.

He hands the palm to BOBIN.

Here, hold it a minute while I . . . I've got cramp.

VÉZINET. It's very modern here. For a marriage room. (*Pointing to the counter.*) This is the witness rail. (*Pointing to the ledger.*) And that's the register. We all have to sign.

BOBIN (*wrestling with the palm*). What about those who can't write?

NONANCOURT. They make their mark.

He examines the dummy with the hat.

Some kind of statue. Modern art. They have that here, you know.

BOBIN. The Town Hall at home's much better.

HÉLÈNE. What happens next, Papa?

FADINARD. Nay, lass. You lower your eyes, you say, 'I do', it's done.

BOBIN. 'I do, it's done'. Oh. (*Passing* VÉZINET *the palm.*) Hold this while I blow my nose.

VÉZINET. A pleasure. I was just blowing my nose. (*Passing it to* NONANCOURT.) Hold this a minute.

NONANCOURT. I should have left it in the cab.

Enter TARDIVEAU, *with the ribbons round his neck.*

TARDIVEAU. Golly, it's hot.

NONANCOURT. It's the mayor. Look, with his sashes. Keep your gloves on.

BOBIN (*aside to him*). Uncle, I've lost one.

NONANCOUNRT. Put your hand in your pocket. (*As* BOBIN *puts the gloved hand in his pocket.*) The other one. Oaf.

BOBIN *puts both hands in his pockets.* TARDIVEAU *has gone behind the counter and found his cotton jacket.*

TARDIVEAU. At last I can change.

NONANCOURT *presents* HÉLÈNE *to him.*

NONANCOURT. This is the bride, your Honour. (*Aside to her.*) Curtsey.

HÉLÈNE *curtseys.*

TARDIVEAU (*putting his cotton jacket out of sight*). What's this in aid of?

NONANCOURT (*proudly*). This is my daughter.

BOBIN. And my cousin.

NONANCOURT. I'm her father.

BOBBY. And I'm her cousin.

NONANCOURT. And these are all our relations. (*To the others.*) Say good morning, then.

The GUESTS *all bow and curtsey, and* TARDIVEAU *bows left and right to them.*

TARDIVEAU (*aside*). They're very polite. I'll change when they've gone.

NONANCOURT. How do you start? D'you take our names?

He puts the palm on the counter.

TARDIVEAU. Well, it's not the usual thing, but . . . (*Aside as he opens the ledger.*) A country wedding party, come to buy hats. Better humour them.

NONANCOURT. Ready? (*Dictating.*) An-toine . . . Petit-Pierre . . .

TARDIVEAU. We don't need Christian names.

NONANCOURT. Really? (*To the others.*) At home, they insist on them.

TARDIVEAU. Please hurry up. I'm boiling.

NONANCOURT. Sorry. (*Dictating.*) Antoine, Petit-Pierre, Voiture, Nonancourt (*Wriggling his foot.*) Ee-ow-ouch. I'm sorry. My shoe. It pinches. (*Beckoning to* HÉLÈNE.) Your turn, lass.

HÉLÈNE. Papa, it's still sticking into me.

TARDIVEAU. Monsieur, we're wasting time. (*Aside.*) I'll *melt!* (*Aloud.*) Your address.

NONANCOURT (*proudly*). M.W.S.M.G.S.D.

BOBIN (*eagerly*). Member of the Worshipful Society of Market Gardeners, Seedsmen and Dibblers.

TARDIVEAU. We don't need that.

NONANCOURT. Born at Grosbois, 7 December, Oh-seven.

TARDIVEAU. I didn't ask for an autobiography.

NONANCOURT. Sorry, I'm sure. (*To the others.*) High and mighty, isn't he? (*To* VÉZINET.) Your turn.

Pause. VÉZINET *takes no notice.* BOBIN *pushes him forward.*

BOBIN. Your turn.

VÉZINET *advances majestically to the counter.*

VÉZINET. Your Honour, before I agreed to be a witness –

TARDIVEAU. Pardon?

VÉZINET. – I took the trouble to find out my duties.

NONANCOURT. Where the devil's my son-in-law?

VÉZINET. There are, so far as I can see, three main requirements in a witness –

TARDIVEAU. But we don't –

VÉZINET. The first, and most important –

BOBIN *has opened the door to the workroom.*

BOBIN. Uncle! Look!

NONANCOURT. What? Galloping geraniums, my son-in-law, kissing another woman.

GUESTS. Oh!

Pandemonium.

BOBIN. The bounder.

HÉLÈNE. The beast.

NONANCOURT. On his wedding day!

VÉZINET (*continuing, oblivious*). The second is to be French born, or at least naturalised . . .

NONANCOURT (*to* TARDIVEAU). That's enough. It's all off. Cross it all out. I'm taking my daughter back. Bobin can have her.

BOBIN (*delighted*). Oh, Uncle.

Enter FADINARD.

GUESTS. Oh. Here he is. Bounder. Swine.   [MUSIC 6]

FADINARD. What's the matter with you? Why didn't you wait in the cabs?

NONANCOURT. Son-in-law, it's all off.

FADINARD. Naturally.

NONANCOURT. It's like the orgies of ancient Rome. Lobelias to you, Monsieur.

BOBIN *and* GUESTS. Lobelias! Lobelias!

FADINARD. But what have I done?

GUESTS. Oh!

NONANCOURT. I've just caught you at it. Lobelias!

FADINARD (*aside*). Blast. He saw. (*Aloud.*) I deny . . . nothing.

GUESTS. Oh!

HÉLÈNE (*in tears*). He admits it. Waaaah.

BOBIN. There, there, cousin. (*To* FADINARD.) Lobelias!

FADINARD. That's enough . . . and keep off the grass.

BOBIN. She is my cousin.

NONANCOURT. It's perfectly harmless.

FADINARD. Exactly. And the lady I was kissing just now is . . . *my* cousin.

GUESTS. Oh!

NONANCOURT (*taking this in his stride*). That's grand. Introduce us. I'll invite her to the wedding.

FADINARD (*aside*). Wonderful. (*Aloud.*) No point. She never goes out. She's in mourning.

NONANCOURT. In a pink dress?

FADINARD. It's for her husband . . .

NONANCOURT. Right. (*To* TARDIVEAU.) It's all on again. Bobin, give her back.

BOBIN (*muttering*). Lobelias.

NONANCOURT. We'll start again. Sit down, everyone, sit down.

They all sit down in front of TARDIVEAU.

FADINARD (*aside*). Now what are they doing . . . ?

TARDIVEAU. I've had enough of this.

He picks up his cotton jacket and starts to go.

NONANCOURT. Where's he off to? Some kind of side room?

TARDIVEAU. I must get changed.

Exit.

NONANCOURT. After him. His Worship. Don't let him get away.

They all go after TARDIVEAU.   [MUSIC 7]

FADINARD *is alone onstage.*

FADINARD. What *is* going on?

Enter CLARA.

CLARA. There you are.

FADINARD. Ah, Clara.

CLARA. Here's your sample back. I can't match it.

FADINARD. What?

CLARA. The straw's too fine. You'll never find one like it.

FADINARD (*aside*). Now what?

CLARA. If you don't mind waiting a fortnight, I can order you one from Florence.

FADINARD. A fortnight.

CLARA. Round here, I've only ever seen one like it.

FADINARD. I'll buy it.

CLARA. It's not for sale. I sent it eight days ago to the
    Duchess of Champigny.

FADINARD (*pacing, while* CLARA *potters*). A Duchess. You
    can't just stroll up and say, 'OK, Duchess, how much for
    the hat?' Oh well, hard luck on Napoleon and his
    girlfriend. I'll just get married, and then I'll –

TARDIVEAU (*hurrying in, still carrying his cotton jacket*). Golly,
    it's hot.

The entire wedding party follows him across the stage. [MUSIC 8]

*When he sees them, he hurries out at the other side, and they all go
after him.*

CLARA. What *is* going on?

She hurries after them.

FADINARD. What are they playing at? Nonancourt! Father-
    in-law! Just a minute . . .

Enter FÉLIX *from the street.*

FÉLIX. Monsieur. Monsieur. I've just come from home.

FADINARD. Where's the soldier?

FÉLIX. Swearing, grinding his teeth, breaking chairs . . .

FADINARD. Oh, God . . .

FÉLIX. You've planned the whole thing, he says. Your ten
    minutes are up. He's going to deal with you, he says. He's
    going to wait, and deal with you.

FADINARD. Félix, this is what I want you to do. Pick him up, and throw him out the window.

FÉLIX. He won't like that.

FADINARD. What's the lady doing?

FÉLIX. Hysterics. Sobbing. Sniffing.

FADINARD. Tell her to blow her nose.

FÉLIX. We sent for the doctor. He put her straight to bed.

FADINARD. What bed? Whose bed?

FÉLIX. Well, yours, Monsieur.

FADINARD (*beside himself*). I won't have that. I won't have that. My wife's own wedding couch! I won't have that. Sobbing, sniffing . . . Go back, make her get up, and change the sheets.

FÉLIX. But Monsieur –

FADINARD. Tell them I've found . . . the Object.

FÉLIX. What . . . Object?

FADINARD. Go on.

He pushes him out.

That finishes it. Hysterics, a doctor, a madman smashing chairs. I've got to get that hat. Wherever it is. Crowned head. Top of the Arc de Triomphe. Oh, my God, the wedding guests? I'll never get them up there.

Enter CLARA, gazing offstage in astonishment. He grabs her.

Clara. Quick. Where does she live?

CLARA. Who?

FADINARD. The Duchess.

CLARA. Which Duchess?

FADINARD. The one with the hat, idiot.

CLARA. Idiot?

FADINARD. No, no. Angel, I meant angel. Give me her address.

CLARA. Tardiveau can take you. He's just coming. Wait. Will you marry me?

FADINARD. Wait and see.

Enter TARDIVEAU, *at his wits' end.*

TARDIVEAU. What is it they *want*? And why can't I *change*?

CLARA. Quick. Take Monsieur to the Duchess of Champigny.

TARDIVEAU. But −

FADINARD. Hurry up. I've got a cab outside. Eight cabs. Come *on*!

He hurries him out. The wedding party appears and hurries after them as the curtain falls.   [MUSIC 9]

End of Act Two.

ACT THREE

The magnificently furnished and decorated salon of the DUCHESS
OF CHAMPIGNY. *Grand piano. Main entrance, right. Double
doors, centre, open on to a dining room set for a superb buffet: this can
be seen as the curtain rises. Left, doors open to the rest of the chateau.
Luxury and elegance. Enter* ACHILLE DE ROSALBA.

ACHILLE. I say. Amazing, weally amazing. What a
wonderful supwize.

Enter DUCHESS.

DUCHESS. Dear boy . . .

ACHILLE. Auntie, this is weally delightful. A musical
matinée, the invitation said, and everything's laid weady
for a supper party.

DUCHESS. But of course. We'll have the concert first, then
supper, and after supper, dancing.

ACHILLE. Huwwah! And at the concert, Auntie: will there
be singers?

DUCHESS. But of course. Why do you ask?

ACHILLE. You know me, Auntie. I wote a little song this
vewwy morning.

DUCHESS (*aside*). Ffff.

ACHILLE. 'Bweeze of evening.'

DUCHESS. How original.

ACHILLE. Imagine the scene. Pastowal. Haymaking. A handsome young shepherd, welaxing on the gwass . . .

DUCHESS. Tomorrow, perhaps. At whist. Today, we have singers from Italy, opera-singers, great talents. That tenor from Milan, Nisnardi.

ACHILLE. Don't wemember *him*.

DUCHESS. He's only been eight days in Paris. Everyone's inviting him, everyone.

ACHILLE. Still don't wemember him.

DUCHESS. I wasted no time. Yesterday, I sent him a note. Three thousand francs, to sing two songs.

ACHILLE. He could have sung 'Bweeze of Evening' for nothing.

DUCHESS. He'd have been insulted. This morning, his answer came.

ACHILLE. How Italian!

DUCHESS. 'Dear-a laidy, You ask-a me seeng two songs, I seeng-a three. You offer three thousand'a franc. Ees not enough.'

ACHILLE. I say.

DUCHESS. 'I ask-a . . . one rose from your corsage.'

ACHILLE. I say. I must put that in a song.

DUCHESS. Such a charming man! Last week he sang for the Countess of Bray. You know her? Such charming . . . feet.

ACHILLE. I know.

DUCHESS. And do you know what he asked of her?

ACHILLE. A wubber plant?

DUCHESS. A slipper. A dancing slipper.

ACHILLE. How quaint.

DUCHESS. Original.

ACHILLE. What will the fellow ask for next?

DUCHESS. Achille!

ACHILLE. Sowwy, Auntie. But these tenor chappies are all the same.

Noises, off.

DUCHESS. Surely not my guests already? Dear boy, I rely on you. Excuse me.

Exit.

ACHILLE. Wely on me, Auntie. Wely on me.

Enter BUTLER.

BUTLER. There's a gentleman outside to speak with Her Ladyship.

ACHILLE. What's his name?

BUTLER. He refused to give his name. He said he communicated with Her Ladyship this morning.

ACHILLE (*aside*). It's him. The tenor. The slipper-chappie. The fellow who turns down thwee thousand fwancs. A fellow-musician. A fellow toiler of the Muses. I'm agog! (*To the* BUTLER.) Show the fellah in.

The BUTLER *turns to go, as* FADINARD *comes in. They collide.*

FADINARD. Sorry, sorry.

Exit BUTLER. FADINARD *hasn't seen* ACHILLE.

What a place! Furniture, curtains, pictures. Look at them. Ancestors. 'Who the devil are you, sir? This isn't a hat-shop. Out!' (*shivers.*) Brrr.

ACHILLE (*examining him from a distance*). Obvious Italian. The way they *dwess*! Haw haw haw.

FADINARD (*starting at the sound*). Aah! Who's this? Another butler? (*Bowing several times.*) Monsieur, monsieur, monsieur.

ACHILLE. Sit down, what?

FADINARD. I've done that. I mean, in the cab. Just now.

ACHILLE. You came by cab? Owiginal.

FADINARD. Uncomfortable.

ACHILLE. But then, you're an owiginal yourself. Fond of a weally tasty foot?

FADINARD. Jellied or boiled?

ACHILLE. Haw haw. Dancing-slipper, eh? Haw haw.

FADINARD (*aside*). What's he talking about? (*Aloud.*) Ahem, if it's not too much trouble, I'd like a moment with the Duchess.

ACHILLE. It's incwedible. You haven't the slightest accent.

FADINARD. Too kind . . .

ACHILLE. I mean, you could have been born in *Weims*.

FADINARD. Weims? Oh, Reims. I'm sorry, if it's not too much trouble, I'd like a moment with −

ACHILLE. Her Ladyship will be down diwectly. In the meantime, allow me to welcome you. Achille, Viscount Wosalba. At your service.

FADINARD (*bowing a lot, aside*). A Viscount. I can't ask these people for a hat.

ACHILLE. I say . . .

FADINARD. Your Highness?

ACHILLE *puts his arm round his shoulders.*

ACHILLE. What would you say to a little thing, the mee-west twifle, 'Bweeze of Evening'?

FADINARD. I . . . well, I . . . pardon?

ACHILLE. Pastowal. Hay-making. Young shepherd, welaxing on the gwass . . .

FADINARD (*disengaging himself*). I'm sorry, but if it's not too much trouble, I really would like −

ACHILLE. Wight away. I'll tell her you've awwived. Excuse me.

FADINARD. No, no, excuse me.

ACHILLE. Not the slightest accent. Haw haw haw.

Exit.

FADINARD. I thought I'd never get here. At least they're
expecting me. I sent her a note. From Clara's. 'Your
Highness, two heads are attached to your hat. As the
proverb says, a stitch in time, what what?' They all talk like
that, 'What, what?' I signed it 'Lord Fadinard'. They all do
that. What *is* she doing? They're all waiting outside, the
wedding guests. Needless to say, they insisted on coming.
All of them. Father-in-law, that warthog . . . nose pressed
to the window, shouting, 'Son-in-law! Son-in-law! Whose
statue is that? What street is that? Where's this now?
Where are we going?' To shut him up, I said we were
going to a country hotel for the reception. So where do you
think he thinks we are? I thought you would. He does. I've
asked them not to let them in. I can't let the Duchess see
them. What a *time* she's taking. If she knew I'd two lunatics
at home, smashing up the furniture . . . By tonight, there
won't be a chair in the place to offer my darling wife. Oh,
yes. I ought to mention that. Small detail. We did it on the
way. Tied the knot. Well, father-in-law was foaming at the
mouth. Hélène was crying. Bobin was . . . well, he was . . .
Anyway, I found a registry office in a traffic-jam, and got it
all over. Dear Hélène. You should have seen her. An angel,
a turtle-dove. What is the woman *doing*?

Enter DUCHESS. *She is wearing a ballgown and carries roses.*

DUCHESS. Signor.

FADINARD (*starting*). Aah!

DUCHESS. I've kept you waiting.

FADINARD. No, no, I . . . (*Aside.*) I can't go through with this.

DUCHESS. I'm so glad you came early. Time to talk. You're not cold, are you? You're shivering.

FADINARD. I did come by cab.

DUCHESS. That's one thing I can never give you. The Italian weather.

FADINARD. I wouldn't know what to do with it. I'd rather have . . . something else.

DUCHESS. What a magnificent country, Italy.

FADINARD. Yes. Yes. (*Aside.*) *Why?*

DUCHESS. Its palaces . . . its hills . . . its vineyards . . .

FADINARD. Its straw hats.

[*Original replaced the last two speeches with* MUSIC 10.]

DUCHESS. Pardon?

FADINARD. Your Highness, you did . . . you must have . . . that is, the note I wrote this morning . . .

DUCHESS. I cherish it!

She sits, and beckons him to fetch a chair.

FADINARD. You don't think . . . I wasn't . . . it wasn't . . . *forward* at all?

DUCHESS. Silly boy, of course not.

FADINARD (*fetching a chair and sitting*). I mean, it *is* true. A stitch in time . . .

DUCHESS. Pardon?

FADINARD. Saves nine.

DUCHESS. I do believe it does. (*Aside.*) Tenors know everything.

FADINARD (*aside*). She's had it. She's read it. She'll give me the hat.

DUCHESS. Ah, music. What a joy!

FADINARD. Eh? I mean, ah.

DUCHESS. Such fire, such passion, such emotion.

FADINARD. Oh, yes. Especially . . . hat music. (*Aside.*) That should do it.

DUCHESS. Tell me, do you ever play Rossini?

FADINARD. That's not my game. (*Aside.*) What *now*? (*Aloud.*) Your Highness, my letter . . .

DUCHESS. I'll cherish it forever.

FADINARD. Why?

DUCHESS. Tell me: how high would you put *The Barber*?

FADINARD. High enough to reach, of course. Your Highness, in the note, I asked, I begged –

DUCHESS. Of course! How silly of me. You really *do* insist . . . ?

FADINARD (*jumping up, eagerly*). Oh, yes! (*More restrained.*) I mean: Oh, yes.

DUCHESS. You people are *so* hot-blooded.

She goes to the piano.

It would be cruel to keep you waiting a moment longer.

FADINARD (*aside*). I'll take the blasted thing, and go. Should I offer to pay? Should I bargain? No, no – a Duchess.

The DUCHESS *ceremoniously hands him a single rose.*

DUCHESS. There you are, signor. Payment in full.

FADINARD (*aside*). She can't have got my note. I'll sue the postman.

[*In the original, there follows a musical scene:* MUSIC 11. *It is replaced here by dialogue. The original dialogue resumes at the line* 'You know I'll refuse you nothing', page 47.]

DUCHESS. Now, what are you going to sing for us?

FADINARD. Sing?

DUCHESS. Come, come, you know how eager we all must be. The great Nisnardi.

FADINARD (*aside*). I'm lost again.

DUCHESS. You must charm and delight us, as you charm and delight audiences all over the world.

FADINARD (*aside*). Audiences? Nisnardi. Ah, they think I'm . . . (*Aloud.*) Your Highness . . . (*Aside.*) If I want that hat, I'll have to humour her. (*Aloud.*) Nisnardi. Hahaha. (*Aloud.*) Got it! (*Aloud.*) Your Highness . . .

DUCHESS. Signor?

FADINARD. Just one request, before your guests arrive.

DUCHESS. Anything, signor.

FADINARD. I hardly dare to ask.

DUCHESS. Oh, dare, dear boy, dare. You know I'll refuse you nothing.

FADINARD. It's just that . . . it may seem . . . a little unusual.

DUCHESS (*aside*). Not my dancing-slipper.

FADINARD. It's my voice. Artistic temperament. It knows what it needs . . . and when it needs it –

DUCHESS. It has to have it?

FADINARD. Exactly. Or it goes. It just . . . (*Hoarsely.*) goes. Hoo-hoo. Haargh. Refuses to sing a note.

DUCHESS (*aside*). I knew it! (*Aloud.*) My dear signor! What does it want, your voice?

FADINARD. It's rather unusual.

DUCHESS. A whole bouquet?

FADINARD. Even more unusual.

DUCHESS (*aside*). I'm sorry I invited him.

FADINARD. Your Highness's hair is very pretty.

DUCHESS. My hair! Oh, no!

FADINARD. It makes me think of that hat you were wearing yesterday.

DUCHESS. At the races?

FADINARD. That's right. Such a gorgeous hat, such a ravishing hat.

DUCHESS. You mean it's the hat?   [MUSIC 12]

Haw haw haw.

FADINARD. Haw haw. (*Aside.*) It's working!

DUCHESS. It's the slipper all over again.

FADINARD. What slipper?

DUCHESS. Haw haw haw.

FADINARD. Haw haw. (*Aside.*) What slipper?

DUCHESS. Don't worry, signor. You can have the hat.

FADINARD. Ah.

DUCHESS. I'll send it tomorrow.

FADINARD. No, now! I need it now!

DUCHESS. But surely . . .

FADINARD. My voice . . . hoo-hoo, haargh . . .

DUCHESS. Oh, dear.

She rings the bell

Clotilde! Clotilde!

Enter MAID. *The* DUCHESS *says something urgently to her, and she goes.*

Five minutes. Five minutes, you'll have it in your hands. I'm sorry, but a hat . . . It's so original! Haw haw haw haw.

Exit, laughing.

FADINARD. Five minutes. I'll have the hat, I'll be out of this madhouse. I'll leave my purse to pay for it. Ha! Nonancourt! Father-in-law! He must be tearing his hair, out there in the cabs.

Enter NONANCOURT, *with a napkin under his chin.*

NONANCOURT. Where the devil's my son-in-law?

FADINARD. Erk!

NONANCOURT (*slightly tipsy*). Son-in-law, it's all off.

FADINARD. What are you doing here?

NONANCOURT. Having dinner. What d'you think I'm doing?

FADINARD. Where?

NONANCOURT. In there.

FADINARD (*aside*). The buffet. Haaaargh!

NONANCOURT. Nice lil hotel. I'll come here again.

FADINARD. I'm sorry, you –

NONANCOURT. And so you should be. Your manners are incredible.

FADINARD. What d'you mean?

NONANCOURT. Deserting your wife on her wedding day. Letting her eat dinner without you.

FADINARD. You mean, *she's* in there?

NONANCOURT. They're all in there. Stuffing their faces.

FADINARD. I've gone all . . . I feel a bit . . .

He wipes his brow with NONANCOURT'*s napkin.*

NONANCOURT. You too? I don know, I feel a lil bit −

FADINARD. What about the rest of them?

NONANCOURT. Wonderful time. Bobin started a game of
Hunt the Slipper. Laugh? You should have heard us.
(*Wriggling his foot.*) Ee-ow-ouch.

FADINARD (*aside*). For Heaven's sake where is that hat?

GUESTS (*off*). Long live the bride! Long live the bride!

FADINARD (*at the door*). Shhh! For Heaven's sake,
shhhhhhhh!

NONANCOURT (*who has collapsed onto the sofa*). D'you know, I
can't think *where* I put that potted palm.

FADINARD (*rushing to him*). Oh, God. Get in there, now!

He stuffs the napkin into his top pocket, and starts trying to get
NONANCOURT *out of the room.*

NONANCOURT (*resisting*). You don't understand. I potted it
the day she was born.

FADINARD. It's in the cab. The cab!

Enter BUTLER *with a candelabrum. He opens the door to the
dining room, and we see the* GUESTS *having a wonderful time.*

BUTLER. Hey!

FADINARD. Oh, God!

He drops NONANCOURT, *who collapses back on the sofa.*

FADINARD *grabs the butler, snatches his candelabrum and bundles him into a cupboard.*

Get in there. Don't make a sound. Or else. Or . . . ELSE!

Enter DUCHESS.

Your Highness.

DUCHESS. What are you doing with all those candles?

FADINARD. My hanky. I was looking for my hanky.

DUCHESS. Haw haw haw.

FADINARD. Pardon?

DUCHESS. It's there, in your pocket. Haw haw haw.

FADINARD. So it is. Haw haw.

DUCHESS. Well, signor, did they bring you what you wanted?

FADINARD (*desperately trying to hide* NONANCOURT *from view*). Not yet, your Highness. And I need it, I need it.

NONANCOURT. D'you know, I think I'm a lil bit –

DUCHESS. Who is this gentleman?

FADINARD. He accompanies me everywhere.

He hands the candelabrum to NONANCOURT, *who cradles it.*

DUCHESS (*to* NONANCOURT). Congratulations, Monsieur. It must be most demanding, being an accompanist.

NONANCOURT. Eh?

FADINARD (*Aside to him*). She thinks you're my . . . oh, never mind.

NONANCOURT. Hello there. (*Aside to* FADINARD.) Bit lah-dee-dah. Did you invite her?

FADINARD (*aside*). Where *is* that *hat*?

DUCHESS. Are you Italian, too?

NONANCOURT. I'm from Charentonneau.

FADINARD. Ciarentonnaio. Near Milan. You know.

NONANCOURT. D'you know, I really miss that potted palm.

DUCHESS. What potted palm?

FADINARD. It's a new song. 'The Potted Palm'. Very . . . potted.

DUCHESS (*to* NONANCOURT). Would you like to try the piano? It's a concert grand.

NONANCOURT. Beg pardon?

FADINARD. It's hopeless.

DUCHESS. And I hope you'll both stay for dinner, afterwards.

NONANCOURT. You're very kind, but no. I've had enough for now.

DUCHESS. Well, come along. My guests. I'll see if they've arrived. They'll be so *pleased* to meet you.

NONANCOURT. More guests? What a wedding.

DUCHESS. Your arm, Monsieur?

NONANCOURT (*aside to* FADINARD). Oh, lah-dee-dah.

FADINARD (*in despair*). Dee-dah.

NONANCOURT (*to the* DUCHESS, *as they go*). I must have
    put it *somewhere.* I mean, a potted palm . . .

Exeunt. FADINARD *collapses on the sofa.*

FADINARD. Oh God, oh God, oh God, oh God. They'll
    throw us all out.

Enter MAID, *with a hatbox.*

MAID. Here's the hat, Monsieur.

FADINARD. At last! the hat!

He takes the box, and kisses her.

MAID. Monsieur!

FADINARD. Here, my purse. You can have that too.

MAID. What's wrong with him?

FADINARD. It's mine. At last! It's mine.

He opens the box, and takes out a black silk hat with a long veil.

What? Silk?

He throws it down, and grabs the maid.

Here, you. The other one. Quick, the other one.

MAID. Signor, signor, you're hurting me.

FADINARD. The Italian straw hat. Where is it?

MAID. Her Ladyship gave it to her god-daughter. Madame
    Beauperthuis.

FADINARD. Thunder and lightning. Where does *she* live?

MAID. In Paris. 12, Rue de Ménars.

FADINARD. Good. Right. Shoo!

The MAID *takes the hat and scurries out.*

I'll go there. The guests, Nonancourt. Oh, let them sort it out!

[*Translator's note: from here to the end of the act, the original had a music number involving the Duchess's* GUESTS: MUSIC 13. *It is replaced here by dialogue.*]

He starts to go. BOBIN *pokes his head round the door.*

BOBIN. Cousin.

FADINARD. What?

BOBIN. Is there going to be dancing?

FADINARD. Oh, yes. When the music starts.

BOBIN *goes in and shuts the door.*

Now then, 12 Rue de Ménars . . .

He is about to go, when the DUCHESS *and* NONANCOURT *return.*

DUCHESS. Ah, there you are.

NONANCOURT. She's crazy, son-in-law. Keeps on and on about Italy.

DUCHESS. It's most peculiar. My guests are waiting outside. Apparently the footmen won't let them into the house.

FADINARD. Ah. I can explain.

DUCHESS. You are Nisnardi, aren't you?

NONANCOURT. Nisnardi? What's one of those?

FADINARD (*wearily*). Singer. Songs.

NONANCOURT. A singsong? Just what we need, a singsong. Wait a moment . . .

He goes to the piano.

FADINARD. You can't play the piano.

NONANCOURT. I'll have a damn good try.

He starts thumping the piano. Cheers from the dining-room.

FADINARD. That's done it.

BOBIN *opens the doors and ushers in the* WEDDING-GUESTS.

BOBIN. Come on, the music's started. In here, everyone.

DUCHESS. What on Earth . . . ?

FADINARD. It's all right.

DUCHESS. Who are all these people?

FADINARD (*backing away*). I can explain . . . I can explain everything . . .

The BUTLER *leaps out of the cupboard and grabs him.*

BUTLER. Got you!

FADINARD. It's no use. Women and children first!

He rushes out.

BOBIN. It's another game. Quick, after him!

He and the GUESTS *rush out. The* DUCHESS *is left alone with* NONANCOURT, *who is still hammering the piano.*

NONANCOURT. I'll try a waltz now . . . Oh, they've gone. (*getting up.*) Hey, missus . . . (*Wriggling his foot.*) Ee-ow-ouch! Come and help me find my potted palm.

He advances on her. She screams and exits.

Funny woman. Never mind, I'll find it on my own.

Exit. Curtain.

End of Act Three.

ACT FOUR

BEAUPERTHUIS' *bedroom. The bed is in an alcove, curtained off. There are doors left, right and centre, as well as the main door, centre. It is evening, and the lamps are lit.* BEAUPERTHUIS *is sitting in front of an ornamental screen, soaking his feet in a mustard bath.*

BEAUPERTHUIS. It's peculiar. Very peculiar. She says to me at seven minutes to nine this morning, 'Beauperthuis, I'm going to buy a pair of suede gloves.' Now it's quarter to ten at night, and she still isn't back. How can it take twelve hours fifty-two minutes to buy a pair of suede gloves? Unless you go to Sweden. I've racked my brains wondering where she is. I've got a splitting headache. I'm soaking my feet in this bath. The maid's been everywhere, all our relatives and friends. No sign of her anywhere. Just a minute! Auntie Grosminet. Perhaps she's there.

He rings a handbell.

Virginie! Virginie!

Enter VIRGINIE *with a kettle of hot water.*

VIRGINIE. Here's the hot water, Monsieur Beauperthuis.

BEAUPERTHUIS. Put it down, then. Listen –

VIRGINIE. Careful. It's boiling.

BEAUPERTHUIS. Can you remember what Madame was wearing when she went out this morning?

VIRGINIE. Her new dress with the buttons, and her pretty Italian straw hat.

BEAUPERTHUIS (*aside*). That hat. Her godmother gave her that. The Duchess. It must have cost 500 francs. To buy suede gloves in!

He pours water into the bath, and winces.

Odder and odder.

VIRGINIE. Yes, Monsieur.

BEAUPERTHUIS. She must have gone visiting.

VIRGINIE. Yes, Monsieur. (*Aside.*) And we all know who.

BEAUPERTHUIS. I want you to go to Madame Gros-minet's . . .

VIRGINIE. In Gros-caillou?

BEAUPERTHUIS. I know she'll be there.

VIRGINIE (*forgetting herself*). And I know she won't.

BEAUPERTHUIS. You *know* where she is?

VIRGINIE (*hastily*). I mean I know she won't be *there*. It's miles away. Monsieur, I've been running round all evening. I'm exhausted. Gros-caillou's miles away.

BEAUPERTHUIS. Take a cab, then. Here's three francs. Hurry.

VIRGINIE. Yes, Monsieur. (*Aside.*) I'll have a cup of tea with my friend downstairs.

BEAUPERTHUIS. Go *on*.

VIRGINIE. I'm going, Monsieur. (*Aside.*) I won't find that hat. Who cares?

Exit.

BEAUPERTHUIS. My head is *splitting*. I should have put more mustard in. (*Through his teeth.*) Oh, Anaïs, if I didn't trust you totally . . .

Knock, off. He beams.

She's here. At last. Come in.

More knocking.

I'm soaking my feet. Just turn the handle. Come in, darling.

Enter FADINARD, *dishevelled, out of breath, depressed.*

FADINARD. Monsieur Beauperthuis?

BEAUPERTHUIS (*aside*). A complete stranger. Who is he? (*Aloud.*) I'm out.

FADINARD. No you aren't. (*Aside.*) I can't take much more. They gave us all a hiding at the Duchess'. I didn't mind, but Nonancourt was furious. He's going to write to the Tourist Board. 'If that's what they call a hotel . . . ' Ridiculous.

BEAUPERTHUIS. Oi. Whoever you are. Clear off.

FADINARD. Thanks. Those stairs. D'you have to live on the sixth floor?

He takes a chair and sits near BEAUPERTHUIS, *who pulls his towel defensively round his legs.*

BEAUPERTHUIS (*furiously*). You can't just burst in here like this. I simply won't stand for it . . .

FADINARD (*lifting a corner of the towel*). No, I see you won't. Don't stop just for me. I won't take long.

He picks up the kettle.

BEAUPERTHUIS. I don't want visitors. I don't feel like visitors. I've got a headache.

FADINARD. Have some more of this.

He pours water.

BEAUPERTHUIS. Ow! Leave that alone!

He snatches the kettle and puts it down.

What d'you want? Who are you?

FADINARD. Fadinard. Léonidas Fadinard. 25. Man of property. Married this morning. Eight cabs downstairs to prove it.

BEAUPERTHUIS. I don't know you from Adam.

FADINARD. Me neither. But that's all right. It's your wife I want.

BEAUPERTHUIS. You know my wife?

FADINARD. Not remotely. But she's got something, an article of clothing, and I've got to have it, and have it now.

BEAUPERTHUIS. What?   [MUSIC 14]

Who is this person?

FADINARD *pours more boiling water.*

Ow! Get out of here.

FADINARD. Not till I've seen your wife.

BEAUPERTHUIS. She's out.

FADINARD. At this time of night? A likely story.

BEAUPERTHUIS. I tell you she isn't here.

FADINARD (*indignantly*). You mean you sit there and let her gallivant at this time of night? Outrageous!

He pours out a lot more water.

BEAUPERTHUIS. That's *hot*!

He snatches the kettle and puts it down on the other side.

FADINARD (*moving his chair round too*). I understand. She's gone to bed. Don't worry. I only want a word. I'll keep my eyes shut . . .

BEAUPERTHUIS *grabs the kettle and dances with fury in the bath.*

BEAUPERTHUIS. Monsieur!

FADINARD. Which way's her bedroom?

BEAUPERTHUIS. Aargh. Ergh. Grrgh. Take that!

He hurls the kettle at FADINARD, *who retaliates by shutting the screen right round him. Only his socks and shoes are left outside, waiting to be put on.* BEAUPERTHUIS *is completely hidden.*

FADINARD. I warned you. I'll go to any lengths . . .

He goes into the bedroom, right.

BEAUPERTHUIS (*inside the screen*). Come back. I'll . . . Just wait till I find my shoes . . .

Enter NONANCOURT, *with his potted palm.*

NONANCOURT. Why did I let her marry him? That warthog. Leaves us all downstairs, and comes up here himself. Still, at least we've arrived at last. The new apartment, the little love-nest. At last I can change my shoes.

BEAUPERTHUIS (*muffled inside the screen*). I said, just wait.

NONANCOURT. In there, is he? Changing. (*Seeing the shoes.*) How thoughtful. He's put some out already.

He puts on BEAUPERTHUIS' *shoes, and leaves his own in their place.*

That's better. Now, what next? The palm. I'm fed up with it. I'll put it in her bedroom.

BEAUPERTHUIS *sticks out his hand and scrabbles for the shoes.*

BEAUPERTHUIS. Just wait. Don't go.

NONANCOURT (*knocking on the screen*). Which way's her bedroom?

BEAUPERTHUIS. Haraagh! Her bedroom! Haraaagh!

NONANCOURT. It's all right, I'll find it.

He goes into the bedroom, centre. Enter VÉZINET.

BEAUPERTHUIS. My feet must have swollen in the bath.
Ee-ow-ouch.

He limps out of the screen and grabs VÉZINET.

Now, you.

VÉZINET (*laughing*). Not now, thanks. I can't dance another
step.

BEAUPERTHUIS. It's another one. There's a gang of them.
Where's the first one gone? Hey, you, what's happened to
your boss?

VÉZINET. Just what I always say.

Crash from the bedroom, right.

BEAUPERTHUIS. He's in there!

He rushes out.

VÉZINET. Another guest I've never seen. And in a dressing-
gown. Are we sleeping here? Suits me . . .

He potters off into the alcove. Enter NONANCOURT, *still with
his palm.*

NONANCOURT. That's her bedroom, all right. But it
occurred to me, I'll need this. When I make my speech.

He puts the palm on the table, and knocks on the screen.

Get dressed again, son-in-law. I'll bring the bride upstairs.

Exit. VÉZINET *wanders downstage.*

VÉZINET. No potty. Can't see one anywhere.

Enter NONANCOURT, *with* HÉLÈNE, BOBIN *and several*
GUESTS.   [MUSIC 15]

HÉLÈNE *is reluctant.*

HÉLÈNE. I can't. I daren't.

BOBIN. Right, cousin. Come down with me.

NONANCOURT. Quiet, Bobin. Your part in this is over, as
soon as she crosses that threshold.

BOBIN. Oh.

NONANCOURT. Come in, my dear. Fear naught. This is
your nuptial hall.

HÉLÈNE *(full of emotion)*. My . . . husband? Is he here?

NONANCOURT. Inside that screen, getting ready for bed.

HÉLÈNE. I'm going.

BOBIN. Yes, cousin. I'll take you.

NONANCOURT. Quiet, Bobin.

HÉLÈNE. Papa, I'm trembling.

NONANCOURT. And so you should be. It's expected. The
done thing. My little ones, this is the time, I think, for me
to give you a few well-chosen words of advice. Son-in-law,
come and stand on my right hand, here. Keep your
dressing-gown on.

HÉLÈNE. No, Papa, no . . .

NONANCOURT. All right, no, stay inside that screen. And
listen hard. Bobin, pass me my palm.

BOBIN. There.

NONANCOURT. My little ones . . .

He blows his nose.

My children . . .

VÉZINET (*coming up to him*). Do *you* know where they keep the potty?

NONANCOURT. In the cellar! Go and drown yourself.

VÉZINET. Just what I always say. Thanks.

He potters away.

NONANCOURT. Where was I?

BOBIN (*full of emotion*). 'In the cellar. Go and drown yourself.'

NONANCOURT. Oh, right.

He changes the palm to his other arm.

My children, it's a father's most heartfelt moment, when he loses the daughter he loves, the hope of his declining years, the prop of his grey hairs . . . (*Knocking on the screen.*) Son-in-law, this tender flower is yours. Love her, cherish her, coddle her. (*Pause.*) Why doesn't he *say* something? (*Continuing.*) And you, my daughter: you see this plant? I potted it the day you were born. Let it be a symbol to you. (*With growing emotion.*) Let its green branches remind you always that you have a father . . . a husband . . . children . . . (*Losing control.*) its green branches . . . children . . . fathers . . . always . . . (*In a different tone.*) You know what I'm trying to say.

This has been punctuated by sniffs from BOBIN *and sobs from the* GUESTS.

HÉLÈNE (*overcome*). Oh, Papa.

BOBIN (*overcome*). Oh, Uncle.

NONANCOURT (*blowing his nose*). I thought I'd say a few words. Now, time for bed.

HÉLÈNE. Papa, don't leave me.

BOBIN. Let's stay with her.

NONANCOURT. Trust me, angel child. I foresaw your anxiety. I ordered fourteen camp beds for the immediate family. The rest can sleep in the cabs.

BOBIN. Oh, Uncle.

Enter VÉZINET, *with a potty.*

VÉZINET. I found one after all.

NONANCOURT. Congratulations. Come on, Hélène. (*Sighing with emotion.*) Aaahh.

BOBIN (*sighing*). Aahh.   [MUSIC 16]

The lady GUESTS *take* HÉLÈNE *to the bedroom, left. She is reluctant.* BOBIN *tries to follow, but* NONANCOURT *hands him the palm and forces him out into the room right.* VÉZINET *has gone into the alcove and closed the curtain.* NONANCOURT *is left, staring indignantly at the screen.*

NONANCOURT. It's so *rude*. He hasn't even moved. I suppose he went to sleep when I was talking.

He flings open the screen.

No one!

He recoils and collides with FADINARD, *who has come in behind him.*

Ouch!

FADINARD (*too preoccupied even to notice him*). She isn't here. I've been all through the apartment. No sign of her.

NONANCOURT. Son-in-law. What's going on?

FADINARD. You again! What are you, father-in-law or flypaper?

NONANCOURT. Now, now. This is no time for that.

FADINARD. Just leave me alone!

NONANCOURT (*following him about*). You're getting too excited. You'll give yourself a temperature. You're sweating, son-in-law.

FADINARD. Oh, go to bed.

NONANCOURT. All right, I will. But in the morning, I'll want a word.

Exit, right.

FADINARD (*pacing*). She isn't here. I searched everywhere. Turned everything out. Hundreds of hats . . . blue, yellow, green, grey, rainbow . . . but not a wisp of straw.

BEAUPERTHUIS *bursts in.*

BEAUPERTHUIS. There he is. He's been all over. Got you!

FADINARD. Put me down.

BEAUPERTHUIS. Don't try to escape. I've got a pistol in each pocket.

FADINARD. Oh, have you?

As BEAUPERTHUIS *is using both hands to hold him, he slips his hands into the pockets, pulls out the pistols and levels them at him.*

BEAUPERTHUIS. Help! Police!

FADINARD (*shouting*). Keep your voice down.

BEAUPERHUIS. Give me back my guns.

FADINARD. Give me your hat. Your hat or your life.

BEAUPERHUIS. What's happened to me tonight must be unique in the annals of civilisation. I'm soaking my feet, waiting for my wife, and a maniac comes in and holds me up with my own guns, demanding a hat with menaces.

FADINARD. You don't understand. Come over here. It's a tragedy. The straw hat my horse ate . . . in the field . . . its owner wandering in the woods with a soldier . . .

BEAUPERTHUIS. What's all that to me?

FADINARD. Don't you see? They're stuck in my house . . . refuse to leave.

BEAUPERTHUIS. But all she has to do is go home, this young widow.

FADINARD. I wish she was a young widow. There's a husband.

BEAUPERTHUIS (*laughing*). You don't say. Hahahaha.

FADINARD. A pig. A warthog. Trampled her underfoot like a peppercorn.

BEAUPERTHUIS. I know the type.

FADINARD. Yes, but we can pay him back. If you'll only help us. We'll show him, the fool, the cuckold. We'll pull the wool over his eyes.

BEAUPERTHUIS. I don't really –

FADINARD. Look. Here's a sample.

He shows him the fragment of hat.

BEAUPERTHUIS. Heavens!

FADINARD. Italian straw . . . poppies . . .

BEAUPERTHUIS (*aside*). It's hers! She's at his house. The suede gloves were a blind.

FADINARD. How much d'you want for it?

BEAUPERTHUIS (*aside*). Now I understand. (*Taking* FADINARD *by the arm.*) Come on, you.

FADINARD. Where to?

BEAUPERTHUIS. Your house.

FADINARD. Without the hat?

BEAUPERTHUIS (*suddenly*). Just a minute!

He listens at the bedroom door, centre. VIRGINIE *comes in at the main door.*

VIRGINIE. I've been to Gros-caillou, Monsieur. No sign of her.

FADINARD (*aside*). The hat-woman's maid!

VIRGINIE (*aside*). Félix's boss!

BEAUPERTHUIS (*over his shoulder*). Someone's talking in my
  wife's bedroom. Perhaps she's come back. We'll soon find
  out. (*Wriggling his foot.*) Ee-ow-ouch! These shoes do pinch.

He limps into the bedroom.

FADINARD. What are you doing here?

VIRGINIE. I work here.

FADINARD. Work here? For him?

VIRGINIE. What's wrong with that?

FADINARD (*aside*). Oh, no. *He's* the husband. And I've told
  him everything.

VIRGINIE. Has Madame come home, then?

FADINARD. Go away. Or else, or else, or else.

He pushes her out.

The hat . . . the hat I've been chasing all day . . . with my
wedding guests panting behind me . . . the hat I've been
sniffing out like a bloodhound . . . I've got it at last . . .
IT'S THE HAT THAT'S BEEN EATEN!

Screams from the bedroom.

He'll kill her. I'd better –

He is about to rush in, when the door opens and HÉLÈNE *comes
in, in tears and a nightdress, followed by the* GUESTS *and the
bewildered* BEAUPERTHUIS.

GUESTS. Help!

FADINARD. Hélène!

HÉLÈNE. Papa!

BEAUPERTHUIS. Who are all these *people*?

Enter NONANCOURT *and* BOBIN *from the room, right, in nightshirts and nightcaps.*

NONANCOURT *and* BOBIN. What's going on?

BEAUPERTHUIS. Still more of them!

FADINARD. They're all here. That's all I needed.

[MUSIC 17]

BEAUPERTHUIS. What were you doing in there? This is my house . . .

NONANCOURT *and* BOBIN (*astounded*). *Your* house?

GUESTS *and* HÉLÈNE. Oh! Aiee! (*etc.*)

NONANCOURT *marches indignantly on* FADINARD.

NONANCOURT. His house. Not your house. His house.

FADINARD. Father-in-law, you're getting on my nerves.

NONANCOURT. What? You bring us to sleep in a stranger's house? You let your own young bride . . . in a stranger's house? You . . . you . . . Son-in-law, it's all off.

FADINARD. You make me sick. (*To* BEAUPERTHUIS.) You must excuse us, Monsieur. A small mistake . . .

NONANCOURT. Bobin, we'd better get dressed.

BOBIN. Yes, Uncle.

FADINARD. That's right. Then come round to my place. I'll go ahead with my wife.

He goes to HÉLÈNE, *but* BEAUPERTHUIS *pulls him back.*

BEAUPERTHUIS (*pointedly*). Mine still isn't back.

FADINARD. She'll have missed the bus.

BEAUPERTHUIS. She's at your house.

FADINARD. No, no, no. The lady at my house is . . . Mexican. Is she Mexican, your wife?

BEAUPERTHUIS. Do you take me for an idiot?

FADINARD. Just let me think . . .

NONANCOURT. Bobin, where's my jacket?

BOBIN. Here, Uncle.

BEAUPERTHUIS. Where do you live, you?

FADINARD. Live? I don't live.

NONANCOURT. Number Eight, Place –

FADINARD. Don't tell him!

NONANCOURT. Number Eight, Place Baudoyer.

FADINARD. That's done it.

BEAUPERTHUIS. Right, then.

NONANCOURT. Come on, Hélène.

BOBIN. Come on, everybody.

BEAUPERTHUIS (*grabbing* FADINARD). Come on, you.

FADINARD. I keep telling you, she's Mexican.

Exeunt, BEAUPERTHUIS *limping.*   [MUSIC 18]

When the room is quiet, enter VIRGINIE *with a cup and saucer. She goes to the curtained bed in the alcove.*

VIRGINIE. Monsieur, your cocoa.

VÉZINET (*poking his head out*). Just what I always say.

VIRGINIE (*screaming*). Aaahhh!

VÉZINET. That's right. Night-night.

He goes back to bed. Curtain.

End of Act Four.

ACT FIVE

The square outside FADINARD's *house. A street lamp, suspended by a wire over the stage, lights up the frontage of at least one other house; also the guard-post of the Special Constables, and a sentry-box. Eleven o'clock strikes, and a posse of* CONSTABLES *comes out of the guard-post, led by* TROUILLEBERT. TARDIVEAU *is among them.*

TROUILLEBERT. Eleven o'clock. Who's on watch tonight?

CONSTABLES. Tardiveau. Tardiveau.

TARDIVEAU. My dear Trouillebert, I've done three shifts already today, so as to be free tonight. The air gives me a chill.

TROUILLEBERT. How can air give you a chill? You're bald as coot. You 'aven't any 'air.

Laughter from the CONSTABLES.

All right, you lot: truncheons UP, quick MARCH.

Exeunt CONSTABLES.   [MUSIC 19].

TARDIVEAU *takes off his helmet, hangs it up in the sentry-box, and puts on a floppy nightcap.*

TARDIVEAU. That's better. The heat in that station! If
   I've asked Trouillebert once not to put so many logs on,
   I've asked him a hundred times. I'm *dripping*. A cotton
   uniform . . . that's an idea . . .

He unbuttons his tunic, then does it up again.

No, no. There might be ladies passing. (*Holding out his hand.*)
   Oh, really! Rain, now. That's all I need.

*He wraps himself in his cloak and shelters in the sentry-box. Enter
the entire* WEDDING PARTY, *with umbrellas.*
NONANCOURT *has his potted palm, and* BOBIN *is
supporting* HÉLÈNE. VÉZINET, *who has no umbrella, is taking
shelter wherever he can find it.*

NONANCOURT. This way, everyone. Mind the puddle.

He jumps, and they all follow suit.   [MUSIC 20]

What a wedding! What a wedding!

HÉLÈNE. Papa, where's my husband?

NONANCOURT. You're right. We've lost him.

HÉLÈNE. I'm exhausted.

BOBIN. This isn't fair.

GUEST. My feet are killing me.

NONANCOURT. Ah! *I* changed my shoes.

HÉLÈNE. Papa, *why* did you pay off the cabs?

NONANCOURT. What d'you mean? They've cost three
   hundred francs already. I'm not squandering your
   inheritance on cabs, my lass.

BOBIN. Where are we, Uncle?

NONANCOURT. How the devil should I know? I've been following you.

BOBIN. Oh, no, Uncle. I've been following you.

VÉZINET. Why did we get up so early? Is there to be more dancing?

NONANCOURT. Don't you worry. When I get my hands on Fadinard, there'll be more dancing.

HÉLÈNE. He said to go to his place. Place Baudoyer.

BOBIN. This is some sort of place.

NONANCOURT. But is it *his* place, that's what we want to know. (*To* VÉZINET, *who is sheltering under his umbrella.*) Here, you've been here before. Is this his place?

VÉZINET. Just what I always say.

NONANCOURT. I should have known better than to ask.

TARDIVEAU. Aaaa-CHOO.

NONANCOURT. Bless you. Good heavens, a bobby in a bobblehat. He'll know. Excuse me, Place Baudoyer?

TARDIVEAU. Now then, move along.

NONANCOURT. Is that all they ever say?

BOBIN. Ask him the time.

VÉZINET (*popping up under another umbrella*). A quarter to twelve.

NONANCOURT. There's only one thing for it.

He hammers on one of the house doors – not FADINARD's.

HÉLÈNE. Papa, what are you doing?

NONANCOURT. Asking for information. You know how glad people are to help, in Paris.

A CROSS MAN *in a nightcap sticks his head out of the upstairs window.*

CROSS MAN. What d'you want?

NONANCOURT. Place Baudoyer?

CROSS MAN. You bastard.

He hurls a bucketful of water out of the window.
NONANCOURT *jumps out of the way, and* VÉZINET *gets the lot.*

VÉZINET. Lobelias, that's wet.

NONANCOURT. That's Paris.

BOBIN *has climbed up to look at the street sign.*

BOBIN. Uncle! Place Baudoyer. It's here.

NONANCOURT. That's a stroke of luck. Where's number 8?

GUESTS. Here. Let's go in.

NONANCOURT. Hang on. That fool of a son-in-law – he's got the key.

HÉLÈNE. Papa, I'm exhausted. I'm going to sit down.

NONANCOURT. Not on that pavement. You don't know *where* it's been.

BOBIN. There's a light on inside.

NONANCOURT. He must have got back first. (*Hammering and shouting.*) Fadinard! Son-in-law!

GUESTS. Fadinard! Son-in-law!

TARDIVEAU (*picking on* VÉZINET, *who's nearest*). Now then, less noise, now then.

VÉZINET. Not now, thanks.

NONANCOURT (*at the top of his voice.*) Fa-di-nard!

BOBIN. Fine son-in-law you chose.

HÉLÈNE. He's not going to open the door.

NONANCOURT. Fetch a policeman.

ALL. Fetch a policeman.   [MUSIC 21]

In the middle of all this, FÉLIX *comes sauntering down the street.*

FÉLIX. It's a party.

NONANCOURT. His servant. Come here, you.

FÉLIX. His Nibs' wedding party! Excuse me, Monsieur, have *you* seen Monsieur Fadinard?

NONANCOURT. Of course I haven't. Have you?

FÉLIX. I've been looking for the last two hours.

NONANCOURT. I've had enough to last a lifetime. Open the door and let us in.

FÉLIX. I can't, Monsieur. Strict orders. No one in or out. The lady's still inside.

GUESTS. The lady?

NONANCOURT (*savagely*). The *lady*?

FÉLIX. The one without a hat. She's been here all day.

NONANCOURT. That's the giddy limit. On his wedding day – a floozie!

BOBIN. *And* without a hat.

NONANCOURT. Warming her toes at the marital hearth. And what about us . . . his wife, his in-laws? Tramping about for hours on end, with our arms full of potted palms.

He gives VÉZINET *the palm.*

Oh, the shame of it. The shame!

HÉLÈNE. Papa, I think I'm going to –

NONANCOURT. Not on the ground, lass. That dress cost fifty-three francs. My friends, let's shake that warthog's dust off our shoes and go back to Charentonneau.

GUESTS. Charentonneau! Hurray!

HÉLÈNE. But Papa, my wedding presents.

NONANCOURT. Well said. (*To* FÉLIX.) Hey, you. Go in and bring out a hamper, with all my daughter's presents.

FÉLIX. But Monsieur . . .

NONANCOURT. Or else, lad. Or . . . E-E-E-ELSE!

He pushes him inside.

HÉLÈNE. Papa, you've sacrificed me.

BOBIN. Sacrificed her.

NONANCOURT. I thought he was a gentleman. A man of breeding, of property. The swine!

Enter FADINARD, *out of breath.*

FADINARD. Oh boy, oh boy, oh boy, oh boy, oh boy.

GUESTS. It's him!

FADINARD. Good heavens, the wedding. Father-in-law, save me!

NONANCOURT. No. We've had enough. It's all off.

FADINARD. Shh! Listen.

NONANCOURT. Aye? Well?

FADINARD. Shut up!

NONANCOURT. Shut up yourself, warthog!

FADINARD (*after listening for a moment*). No, it's all right. I must have shaken him off. His shoes pinch. He was limping. We've a minute or two left to avoid the massacre.

HÉLÈNE. Massacre?

NONANCOURT. What are you babbling about?

FADINARD. Wait and see. He's got my address. He'll be here any minute, loaded to the gills with swords and pistols. We have to get his wife away.

NONANCOURT. You . . . you Bluebeard.

GUESTS. Bluebeard!

FADINARD. Now what have I done?

Enter FÉLIX *with the presents.*

FÉLIX. Here we are, then.

FADINARD. What did he say?

NONANCOURT. Right. Each of you take one, and let's get going.

FADINARD. What are you doing? Those are the wedding presents. My wife's.

NONANCOURT. They aren't. She's not. She's coming with me, back to Charentonneau.

FADINARD. Wife-napping? At this time of night? I won't have it.

NONANCOURT. You'll have it and like it.

He picks up one of the presents: a hatbox. FADINARD *grabs it.*

FADINARD. Leave that alone.

NONANCOURT. Let go, you bigamist. It's all off, d'you hear, all off!

The hatbox bursts open. He gets the bottom half, and FADINARD *the lid.* VÉZINET *leaps forward.*

VÉZINET. Be careful! That's an Italian straw hat.

FADINARD. What did you say?

VÉZINET. Not now, thanks. Italian. My wedding present. 500 francs. I had to send all the way to Florence for it.

FADINARD (*pulling out his fragment of hat*). Florence? (*Comparing the two.*) It can't be . . . it is! Identical! Identical! Down to the last poppy.

He puts the hat back in the box, and starts jumping for joy, rushing round pumping everyone's hand.

Good old Italy! Hurrah for Italy!

NONANCOURT. He's off his head.

FADINARD. Good old Vézinet. Good old Nonancourt. Good old Hélène. Good old Bobin. (*Shaking* TARDIVEAU's *hand.*) Good old . . . bobby.

TARDIVEAU. Now then, now then.

NONANCOURT (*aside, during this*). A hat worth 500 francs. I'll have that, you warthog.

He removes the hat and shuts the empty box.

FADINARD. I won't be a moment. I'll give her the hat, and throw her out. I won't be a moment . . . not a moment.

He grabs the hatbox and rushes inside.

NONANCOURT. Decree nisi, annulment . . . bravissimo. Come on, everyone, let's find those cabs.

TROUILLEBERT *and the* CONSTABLES *block their way.*

TROUILLEBERT. Now then, now then, where are you taking all those parcels?

NONANCOURT. That's all right. We're moving house.

TROUILLEBERT. At this time of night?

NONANCOURT. You don't understand.

TROUILLEBERT. I think I do. (*To* VÉZINET.) Papers!

VÉZINET. Just what I always say.

TROUILLEBERT. Ho. Comedian, are we?

NONANCOURT. You don't understand. This poor old man is –

TROUILLEBERT. Are you telling me my duty now? Collar him!

The CONSTABLES *collar* NONANCOURT.

HÉLÈNE. That's Papa.

TROUILLEBERT. Not now, Mamzelle. I'll take your statement later.

BOBIN. We can't make statements. We're going to Charentonneau.

TROUILLEBERT. Not tonight you're not. You're coming inside with me. And in the morning, you can all make statements – to the judge.

He gestures to the CONSTABLES, *who hustle them all out.*

NONANCOURT. You can't do this. I know the chief constable! [MUSIC 22]

Exeunt all but TARDIVEAU.

TARDIVEAU. Now it's quiet at last, I'll have a tea-break.

He takes off his uniform cape and hangs it under the helmet in the sentry-box. Meanwhile, FADINARD, ANAÏS *and* ÉMILE *rush out of the house with the hatbox.*

FADINARD. Come *on!* I've got the hat. It's the only thing that'll save you. Your husband knows everything. He's after me. Put on the hat, and go.

He takes the lid off the box. The three of them gaze, transfixed.

Oh.

ANAÏS. Heavens.

ÉMILE. Empty.

FADINARD. It *was* there. My warthog of a father-in-law must've snitched it when I wasn't looking. (*Gazing round.*) Where's he gone? Where's my wife? The wedding guests?

TARDIVEAU (*as he leaves*). In there, mate. Nickered.

Exit.

FADINARD. Nickered? Nickered? Oh, nicked. That means, the hat . . . oh God, now what?

ANAÏS. Disaster.

ÉMILE. Not entirely. I was at school with the Inspector. Just one moment.

Exit into the police-station.

FADINARD. At school with the Inspector. Saved!

A cab draws up offstage.

BEAUPERTHUIS (*off*). This is the place. Wait here.

ANAÏS. My husband!

FADINARD. He took a cab, the cheat.

ANAÏS. I'm going inside again.

FADINARD. Don't do that! He's coming to search the house.

ANAÏS. A-ee!

FADINARD (*pushing her into the sentry-box where* TARDIVEAU's *helmet and cape are hung*). Hide in there. (*Aside.*) So this is married life.

Enter BEAUPERTHUIS, *limping*

BEAUPERTHUIS. Ah, there you are. Thought you'd got away, didn't you? (*Wriggling his foot.*) Ee-ow-ouch.

FADINARD. I went for some cigars. I still need a light. You haven't a light, have you?

BEAUPERTHUIS. Open that door. I insist. And if she's in there, I warn you: I'm armed.

FADINARD. There's the door. Just turn the handle.

BEAUPERTHUIS (*aside*). What's wrong with my *feet* tonight . . . ?

He limps into the house.

FADINARD. This should be fun.

ANAÏS. I'm scared.

FADINARD. No need. He won't find you in there, that's all that matters.

ÉMILE *sticks his head through the upstairs window of the police-station.*

ÉMILE. Quick! Here's the hat.

FADINARD. Saved! Her husband's here. Throw it down, quickly.

ÉMILE *throws the hat, and it catches on the streetlamp.*

ANAÏS. Ah.

FADINARD. Oh.

He jumps up and down, trying to dislodge the hat with his umbrella. Great noise, off, of someone falling downstairs in FADINARD's *house.*

BEAUPERTHUIS (*off*). Eeee-owwwwww!

ANAÏS. Aee!

FADINARD. Oh, boy.

He throws the police cape over ANAÏS *and puts the helmet on her head.*

Don't panic. If he comes too close, just walk up and down, and say, 'Now then, move along, now then.'

ANAÏS. But he'll see the *hat*! Aaahhhh.

She starts walking the beat, up and down. BEAUPERTHUIS *comes out, and* FADINARD *rushes forward and holds the umbrella over his head to stop him seeing the hat.*

FADINARD. Careful. It's raining.

BEAUPERTHUIS. Why don't you leave a light on those stairs?

FADINARD. It's the middle of the night.

Enter ÉMILE *from the police-station.*

ÉMILE. Keep him talking.

He climbs up and starts sawing through the streetlamp wire with his sword.

BEAUPERTHUIS. Leave me alone. It's stopped raining. The stars are out.

FADINARD. You'll still get wet.

BEAUPERTHUIS. You think I'm an idiot.

FADINARD. Whatever you say.

He starts jumping up and down again, trying to dislodge the hat. As he is holding BEAUPERTHUIS's *arm,* BEAUPERTHUIS *is forced to jump too.*

BEAUPERTHUIS. You've got her away somewhere.

FADINARD. What d'you take me for?

BEAUPERTHUIS. Why are we jumping?

FADINARD. To settle my stomach.

BEAUPERTHUIS. For heaven's sake. Constable!

ANAÏS (*aside*). A-ee.

FADINARD. He can't help. (*To* ÉMILE.) Get a move on, can't you? (*To* BEAUPERTHUIS.) He's not allowed to answer. On watch. Secret mission. Interpol.

BEAUPERTHUIS. Let go my arm.

FADINARD. I can't. You'll get soaked.

They jump up and down again. Enter TARDIVEAU.

TARDIVEAU. Hey! Who's in my box?

ANAÏS. Now then, move along, now then.

BEAUPERTHUIS. That was a woman's voice.

FADINARD (*hiding* ANAÏS *with his umbrella*). No, no. A cadet.

TARDIVEAU. What's that on the streetlamp?

FADINARD. Nothing.

BEAUPERTHUIS. Don't give me that.

He breaks free. Desperately, FADINARD *pulls his hat down over his eyes. At the same moment,* ÉMILE *succeeds at last in cutting the wire, and the lamp collapses.*

BEAUPERTHUIS. Help!

TARDIVEAU. Police!

FADINARD. It's all right. It was only a streetlamp collapsing.

BEAUPERTHUIS *struggles with his hat.* CONSTABLES *appear at the door of the police-station, and heads appear at all the house-windows.*   [MUSIC 23]

In the confusion, FADINARD *unhooks the straw hat from the streetlamp and gives it to* ANAÏS, *who puts it on.*

BEAUPERTHUIS (*struggling with his hat*). Help! Help!

He finally gets it off, and finds ANAÏS *glaring at him.*

ANAÏS. So there you are, you warthog!

BEAUPERTHUIS. My wife!

ANAÏS. So this is how you carry on behind my back.

BEAUPERTHUIS. She's got the hat.

ANAÏS. Gallivanting in the streets –

BEAUPERTHUIS. Florentine straw . . .

FADINARD. *And* poppies.

ANAÏS. Leaving me to find my own way home. In the middle of the night. All the way from Cousin Éloise's –

BEAUPERTHUIS. Just a minute. Cousin Éloise –

FADINARD (*interrupting*). She has got the hat.

BEAUPERTHUIS. You went out to buy a pair of suede gloves. It doesn't take fourteen hours to buy a suede gloves.

FADINARD. But she has got the hat.

ANAÏS (*formally to him*). Monsieur, I don't think I've had the pleasure –

FADINARD. No indeed, Madame. But you have got the hat. (*To the* CONSTABLES *and* CITIZENS.) Has she the hat?

CONSTABLES *and* CITIZENS. She's got the hat.

BEAUPERTHUIS. But what about your horse? In the woods?

FADINARD. He's got the hat.

Enter NONANCOURT.

NONANCOURT. Son-in-law, it's all . . . ON!

FADINARD. Allow me to introduce my father-in-law.

NONANCOURT. Félix told me the whole story. It's a credit to you. You're a knight in shining armour. Have my daughter back. Have back the presents. The potted palm. Everything. Just get the others out of jail.

FADINARD (*to* TROUILLEBERT). Officer, if you wouldn't mind . . . My wedding guests?

TROUILLEBERT. Monsieur, a pleasure. (*Shouting.*) Release
the wedding guests!   [MUSIC 24]

Enter WEDDING-GUESTS.

They surround and embrace FADINARD. VÉZINET *suddenly
sees the hat on* ANAÏS's *head.*

VÉZINET. Good heavens!

FADINARD. Get rid of him.

VÉZINET. Look. This lady . . .

BEAUPERTHUIS (*eagerly*). What about her?

VÉZINET. She's got the hat.

BEAUPERTHUIS (*convinced at last*). Ah. I see I was mistaken.
SHE'S GOT THE HAT!

He kisses ANAÏS's *hand. Exeunt omnes in procession.*

[MUSIC 25]

End of the Play.

MUSIC NUMBERS

1. *Page 9, after Fadinard's speech, 'Thankyou, Uncle . . . '*

FADINARD.
> You've got to go.
> I'll miss you so.
> I'll sob and sigh,
> I'll scream and cry,
> But still you've got to go.

VÉZINET.
> I've got to go.
> I know, I know,
> I'd rather stay.
> Life's hard that way,
> But now I've got to go.

2. *Page 9, after Fadinard's line 'Wait till you see her in her wedding dress . . . '*

FADINARD.
> There are ladies all over the town,
> Ladies in, ladies out, ladies up, ladies down,
> Some are high, some are low,
> Some are rather . . . *you* know.
> Some are large, some are small,
> Some are no fun at all –

And they're all outclassed,
They're all surpassed
By my darling, my dear one,
Who'll soon be my near one,
She's marrying me, she's marrying me –

3. *Page 17, after Fadinard's line, 'I need to get my hat . . . '*

NONANCOURT.
    Don't dilly, don't dally,
    Those cabs are here,
    Don't shilly, don't shally,
    It's the wedding of the year.

FADINARD.
    You won't have to wait:
    Don't fret or fear.
    I'd hardly be late
    For the wedding of the year.

HELENE *and* BOBIN.
    Don't dilly, don't dally – *(etc ad lib.)*

4. *Page 27, in stage direction after Fadinard's line, 'Stay where you are.'*

GUESTS.
    Here in these halls sublime -
    They're grand, they're vast –
    We reach the hallowed time –
    At last, at last –
    We'll hear the organ play –
    I can't wait, can you? –
    We'll hear the bridegroom say –
    'I do. Do you?'

5. *Page 28, after Nonancourt's line, 'It's for Hélène.'*

NONANCOURT.

> On the morning she was born,
> My daughter,
> My darling daughter,
> I fetched compost, pot and palm
> And water,
> Lots of water.
> I planted it and tended it,
> Looked after it, defended it,
> Cherished it, nourished it,
> Walked with it, talked with it,
> Watched it grow, watched it shoot,
> Watched it branch, watched it root –

He breaks off because his shoe pinches.

6. *Page 32, after Guests' line, 'Bounder. Swine.'*

GUESTS.

> You cad,
> You're bad,
> You must be mad.

FADINARD.

> But what have I done?
> What's wrong with everyone?

GUESTS.

> You know.
> You're low.
> You so-and-so.

7. *Page 34, in stage direction, after Nonancourt's line, 'Don't let him get away.'*

GUESTS.
> Quick, after him,
> Don't let him get away.
> He knows the place,
> He's on the case,
> Don't let him get away.

8. *Page 35, in stage direction, after Tardiveau's line, 'Golly, it's hot.'*

Reprise of 7.

9. *Page 37, final stage direction.*

Reprise of 7.

10. *Page 44, in place of the two speeches* 'DUCHESS. *Its palaces . . . its hills . . . its vineyards.* FADINARD. *Its straw hats.'*

DUCHESS.
> Take me there, oh take me there,
> To that lovely land beyond compare –

FADINARD.
> Where the hats come from.

DUCHESS.
> Where orange-blossom scents the air,
> Where song-birds chirp and chortle,
> In groves of lime and myrtle,
> Where gondolas take their lazy way
> Across each sunny, hazy bay,
> Where golden cornfields swirl and sway –

FADINARD.
    To grow the straw that makes the hats –

11. *Page 46, after Fadinard's line, 'I'll sue the postman.'*

    The DUCHESS's GUESTS *enter right.*

GUESTS.
    Hello, hello,
    I say, what ho,
    We're jolly glad to be here.
    How do you do?
    How now? What's new?
    Who's this new face we see here?

DUCHESS.
    When I tell you his name
    You'll be happy he came.
    And when you hear
    That voice so dear,
    You'll faint with delight, you'll be happy –

GUESTS.
    It's that singing Italian chappie.

DUCHESS.
    Nisnardi! Nisnardi!

FADINARD.
    Who, me? Who, me?

GUESTS.
    Nisnardi! Nisnardi!

FADINARD.
    Not me. Not me.

DUCHESS.
    He's modest, he's bashful, he's shy.
    He's doing it to tease, to amuse.

FADINARD.
    I'll give it a bit of a try.
    After all, I've got nothing to lose.

(*Spoken.*) All right, ladies, gentlemen: Nisnardi, at your service.

ALL. Signor!

DUCHESS (*spoken*). Dear friends, perhaps while we wait for the rest of the company, you'd care to take a stroll with me in the rose-garden? As soon as everyone's gathered, I know Signor Nisnardi won't disappoint us.

The GUESTS *form a line, and shake* FADINARD's *hand as they move off towards the garden.*

GUESTS.
    Delighted. Charmed.
    How do you do, signor?
    The pleasure's mine.
    Fancy meeting you, signor!

DUCHESS.
    Nisnardi! Nisnardi!

GUESTS.
    Nisnardi! Nisnardi!

FADINARD (*aside, spoken*). I've just had a brilliant idea.

He catches the DUCHESS, *who is about to leave with the last of her* GUESTS.

I wonder if I could have a word, your Ladyship.

DUCHESS. Dear boy.

FADINARD. A favour. A little request. I hardly dare to ask.

12. *Page 48, after the Duchess's line, 'You mean it's the hat?'*

FADINARD.
    It's the hat, it's the hat,
    It's exactly that.
    As soon as I saw it, I yearned for it,
    I ached for it, I burned for it.
    I said, 'It's the hat,
    I must have that hat.'
    I was filled with longing, racked with care,
    I jumped up and down, I tore my hair,
    Just for that, just for that,
    I must have that hat.

13. *Page 54, after Fadinard's line, 'Oh, let them sort it out.'* [*NB Only the verse is sung.*]

He starts to go. BOBIN *sticks his head round the door.*

BOBIN. Cousin.

FADINARD. Yes?

BOBIN. Is there going to be dancing?

FADINARD. Oh yes. As soon as the music starts.

BOBIN goes in and shuts the door.

Now, 12 Rue de Ménars . . .

He dashes out by one door. The DUCHESS *Comes in with* NONANCOURT *at the other.* NONANCOURT *is still giving her his arm, and is still cradling the candelabrum. The* DUCHESS's GUESTS *stream after them, singing.*

GUESTS.
I say, what fun!
This way. Do come along.
Here, everyone.
He's going to sing a song.

DUCHESS. Please take your seats. The concert won't be long.

The GUESTS *find chairs. She takes* NONANCOURT *aside.*

Where's Signor Nisnardi?

NONANCOURT. Search me. (*At the top of his voice.*) Nisnardi!
Nisnardi!

ACHILLE. Here he is!

He comes in, dragging FADINARD.

GUESTS. Bravo!

DUCHESS. Not stage-fright again, Signor?

NONANCOURT (*aside to him*). You're not Nisnardi.

FADINARD. No, no, no, no. (*To the* DUCHESS.) Me, stage-
fright? No, no, no.

GUESTS. Bravo, bravo!

FADINARD (*bowing*). Thankyou, thankyou. (*Aside.*) Trapped in
the very cab!

DUCHESS (*to* NONANCOURT). Take the piano, Signor.

NONANCOURT. Take the piano? Oh, take the piano.

He puts the candelabrum on the piano, and sits.

DUCHESS. Ready, Signor?

FADINARD. What? Oh, ready.

GUESTS. Shh! Shh!

FADINARD (*aside, as he goes to the piano*). Now what do I do? (*Clearing his throat.*) Ahem.

GUESTS. Shh! Shh!

FADINARD (*aside*). Think of something, fast. (*Clearing his throat.*) Aherrrrrm.

GUESTS. Bravo! Bravo!

NONANCOURT. You want a tune? I'll give you a tune.

He pounds the piano tunelessly.

FADINARD (*singing at the top of his voice*). Allons, enfants de la pat –

VOICES (*off*). In there! This way! The dancing!

Enter WEDDING-GUESTS.

NONANCOURT. Son-in-law. Show some manners. Dance with your wife.

FADINARD. Oh, women and children first!

The WEDDING-GUESTS *force the* DUCHESS'S GUESTS *to dance with them. Pandemonium. Curtain.*

End of Act Three

14. *Page 60, after Beauperthuis' line, 'What?'*

FADINARD.
She's got it, I want it, I need the thing so.
I'll wait till I've got it, I simply won't go.
So fetch it now,
I don't care how.
Don't shilly, don't shally,
Don't dilly, don't dally,

Don't fluster and bluster, don't do something rash;
I'm desperate, I'm ruthless, I'll even pay cash.

15. *Page 64, after Vézinet's line, 'No potty. Can't see one anywhere.'*

GUESTS.
This way, my dear.
Your husband's here,
Here in this room
Your gallant groom.
With happy heart
Now play your part.

16. *Page 66, after Bobin's line, 'Aahh.'*

Reprise of 15.

17. *Page 71, after Fadinard's line, 'They're all here. That's all I needed.'*

BEAUPERTHUIS.
It's baffling.
They're here, they're there,
They're everywhere.

NONANCOURT.
It's baffling.
Why all this row?
What's gone wrong now?

FADINARD.
It's baffling.
These wedding guests
Are perfect pests.

BOBIN.
    It's baffling.
    My cousin's scared,
    But I'm prepared.

HELENE.
    It's baffling.
    My wedding night.
    I'm full of fright.

ALL.
    It's baffling.
    Here, there, everywhere,
    Row, now, guests, pests,
    Scared, prepared, night, fright –
    It's baffling.

18. *Page 73, after Fadinard's line, 'I keep telling you, she's Mexican.'*

GUESTS.
    Boo! Boo!
    The shame of it,
    The blame of it,
    The name of it
    Is you! You!
    On the day of your wedding, you run out to play –
    Now we know what you're like, now you're going to pay –

BEAUPERTHUIS.
    That's right!
    The gist of it,
    The wrist of it,
    The fist of it
    Is fight! Fight!

FADINARD.
    There's no need for fighting, there's no need for pain.
    Just calm down and listen, just let me explain . . .

19. *Page 74, after Trouillebert's line, 'Truncheons UP, quick MARCH.'*

CONSTABLES.
    The town's asleep,
    But we're about;
    Our watch we keep,
    So thieves, look out!

20. *Page 75, after Nonancourt's line, 'Mind the puddle.'*

GUESTS.
    Up and down, up and down,
    Up and down across the town,
    Where is that pest?
    When can we rest?

21. *Page 78, after ALL cry, 'Fetch a policeman'.*

GUESTS.
    Fetch a policeman,
    Call a cop;
    This can't go on,
    It's got to stop.

22. *Page 83, after Nonancourt's line, 'I know the chief constable.'*

CONSTABLES.
    Into the nick,
    Be quick.
    Don't argue. Move it.
    March! March! March! March!

GUESTS.
> What do you mean?
> We're clean,
> And we can prove it.

CONSTABLES.
> March! March! March! March!

23. *Page 88, stage direction after Fadinard's line, 'It was only a street-lamp collapsing.'*

ALL.
> What a rumpus, what a riot!
> It's going too far, it's dire, it's steep.
> Shut up, stop it, hush, be quiet!
> There's folk up here who're trying to sleep.

24. *Page 90, after Trouillebert's line, 'Release the wedding guests.'*

GUESTS.
> He's done it!
> He's won it!
> He's got us out of jail.
> We knew it,
> He'd do it,
> We knew he wouldn't fail.

25. *Page 90, final stage direction.*

GUESTS.
> Stand back, make room,
> The bride, the groom,
> Oh, happy day.

VÉZINET.
> Just what I always say.

GUESTS.
　　Sing high, sing low,
　　It's time to go,
　　All trouble past.

NONANCOURT.
　　I'll get some sleep at last.

BEAUPERTHUIS.
　　She's got the hat.

ÉMILE, ANAÏS *and* BOBIN.
　　I'll second that.

TARDIVEAU.
　　Now then, now then.

TROUILLEBERT.
　　I'll tell you when.

FADINARD.
　　When we're old and we're grey,
　　We'll remember this day,
　　We'll gather our loved ones around us and say,
　　'What a wedding that was,
　　What a bedding that was,
　　What a fuss and a bustle, a hustle because
　　Of one silly little, frilly little,
　　Horsy-morsel, pass-the-parcel,
　　Try to track it, change the jacket,
　　Go all arty, sing at party,
　　Don't get flustered, use more mustard –

ALL.
　　ITALIAN STRAW HAT!'